PRAISE FOR SA

"Success is one thing, but wisdom is another. Or so it can seem. Most of us hope for both, even when they seem like rivals. In the case of Terry Looper, success and wisdom have come blessedly together. It wasn't always so. Why and how did things change for him? I enthusiastically urge you to read *Sacred Pace* to hear his story and to grasp his answers. Then I urge you to pursue for yourself the fruitfulness that can come from a transformative process of seeking and hearing from God in relation to all of life's decisions. As Looper so clearly sees, the greatest and surest gift will always be the Giver."

—MARK LABBERTON, PRESIDENT, FULLER THEOLOGICAL SEMINARY

"Terry Looper's story is compelling because he pulls no punches on how hard life can be when we get seriously out of balance. The resulting wisdom that he acquired through those hard times is from God himself—learning to want God's will more than our own! This truth, which is both ancient and contemporary, and the advice he gives as to how to incorporate it in our lives, will be life-giving for those who begin to move at a *Sacred Pace* in the same way Terry has."

—NEWTON CRENSHAW, PRESIDENT, YOUNG LIFE

"Far too many leaders are struggling with the frenetic pace of their lives. The tragic consequences of a life out of control are predictable: deteriorating health, fractured relationships, and unsustainable results. In *Sacred Pace*, Terry Looper offers a better way—born of his own failures and ultimate success. This book can help you live and lead at a higher level!"

—MARK MILLER, INTERNATIONAL BESTSELLING AUTHOR, V.P. HIGH PERFORMANCE LEADERSHIP, CHICK-FIL-A, INC.

"Terry Looper is both a known and unknown spiritual mentor to hundreds of people and organizations, both nationally and internationally. The non-profit where I have been called to serve is thriving today because of Terry's willingness to teach our leadership team the principles for finding God's will that are so brilliantly described in *Sacred Pace*. Reading will take courage, but the results are worth it!"

—VIVIAN SHUDDE, EXECUTIVE DIRECTOR, BROOKWOOD COMMUNITY

"I've done more underlining per page in *Sacred Pace* than in any other book I have ever read. I sincerely believe that *Sacred Pace* is, after the Bible, the most important book I have ever read. My good friend and mentor Terry Looper has written a great book on business, decision-making, and, in no small way, theology. His transparency makes his words all the more meaningful, and his warmth and conversation-like writing style make the whole experience so personal and enjoyable!"

—CHRISTOPHER CRANE, EXECUTIVE CHAIRMAN
AND COFOUNDER OF EDIFY

"As a committed Christian, I thought I had progressed a long way on my spiritual journey—until I read *Sacred Pace*. I saw myself on almost every page, and I expect the insights and concepts in this book will literally change my life. Slowing down and letting the Holy Spirit guide my decision-making seems hard, yet it is immensely freeing. I am putting these insights into action today!"

—DAVID WEEKLEY, CHAIRMAN OF DAVID WEEKLEY HOMES

"My very wise dad's favorite poem was, 'I'd Rather See a Sermon Than Hear One Any Day.' That poem fits Terry Looper well. The world is experiencing a shortage of leaders who walk their talk, but Terry and this magnificent book fill the void to the brim. *Sacred Pace* is the real deal, and you'll find Terry's heartbeat on every page."

—DR. JOE WHITE, CEO AND PRESIDENT OF KANAKUK KAMPS

"From finances to family, the decisions we make in everyday life radically shape who we become. In *Sacred Pace*, Terry Looper lays out a thoughtful, scriptural guide to wise decision-making. This book is for business leaders eager to make sound choices for their organizations, for husbands and wives who want to work together to live Christ-centered marriages, and for fathers and mothers committed to raising up compassionate kids. *Sacred Pace* is north-star wisdom for those who want to make extraordinary decisions in everyday living."

—PETER GREER, PRESIDENT AND CEO OF HOPE
INTERNATIONAL, COAUTHOR OF *MISSION DRIFT*

"I have been absolutely floored by *Sacred Pace!* This book will be a powerful tool for a lot of people, but in my opinion it is *essential* reading for anyone who considers themselves an entrepreneur. If that's you, this book will change your life in profound ways."

—DAVE BLANCHARD, COFOUNDER OF PRAXIS

"How many times have you and I wished God would send us an email or write in the sky His answer for our questions about His will? For the dedicated follower of Christ, it's easy to feel His will is, at times, too mysterious to decipher. That's why this book is so needed. Terry's experience uncomplicates this 'mystery' of finding answers from God for our everyday lives. The simplicity of his four-step process will stick with you and draw you more closely to God's heart!"

—JOE PAULO, PRESIDENT AND CEO OF KSBJ

"This is a book by a thoughtful and successful Christian businessman. He tells the moving story of his own burnout and conversion, but that's only the beginning. Now, after many years of following Christ, Terry Looper shares what he has learned about decision-making as a Christian and connects that with the process of making deals as a businessman. Slowing down and listening (he calls it 'getting neutral') and learning how to sense the leading of the Spirit are insights he has gained from years of business experience and are inextricably linked to his love for Jesus."

—ROBERT SLOAN, PRESIDENT, HOUSTON BAPTIST UNIVERSITY

"I have had the privilege of knowing Terry Looper for the last twenty-five years. I often go to him for wise counsel and advice on a myriad of subjects. He always encourages me to listen the Lord and to get neutral. Reading *Sacred Pace* is just like a visit with Terry, including practical spiritual wisdom that is certainly countercultural. I highly recommend *Sacred Pace* to anyone who runs too fast in this crazy-paced world so they can learn to operate at God's speed."

—TIGER DAWSON, CEO AND PRESIDENT OF EDIFY

"What a fantastic experience it was to read *Sacred Pace!* As I read the first few chapters, I thought the book was good mainly because I have great respect for Terry. At some point in the middle, I realized this book is really good regardless of my thoughts about Terry. And by the end, I have been stimulated to make some life adjustments and think of a few things differently."

—JEFF REETER, NORTHWESTERN MUTUAL, MANAGING PARTNER

"As part of a seminary leadership team, I know how important it is to make decisions in God's timing, rather than our own. The principle of 'getting neutral' that Terry has described in this book is so valuable in that process, which is just one of the reasons I have enjoyed reading *Sacred Pace*."

—TOD BOLSINGER, VICE PRESIDENT, FULLER THEOLOGICAL
SEMINARY, AUTHOR OF *IT TAKES A CHURCH TO RAISE A CHRISTIAN*

"*Sacred Pace* is packed full of godly wisdom. I especially like the way my friend Terry Looper breaks out the application portions of the book based on the major segments of a leader's life—and the way he includes key examples along the way. This is a powerful tool that I know will impact many people's lives."

—LLOYD REEB, AUTHOR OF *FROM SUCCESS TO*
SIGNIFICANCE AND *HALFTIME FOR COUPLES*

"This book has been helpful for my soul. My wife and I read it together at the perfect time, and we've been using Terry's four steps to 'get neutral' in our lives, in our ministry, and in our parenting decisions. This book needs to be in the hands of any young person looking to get a start on life—especially anyone ready to get started in the business world."

—REV. DR. DANA ALLEN, SYNOD EXECUTIVE, ECO

"In *Sacred Pace*, Terry Looper speaks to the longings of our hearts. We long to flourish in every part of life—in business, family, discipleship, and service to others. This book offers a clear path to such flourishing. We yearn for integrated lives, rather than being so scattered. *Sacred Pace* shows us how to live seamlessly, centered in the God who loves us and guides us. We look for a mentor, someone who can help us grow in work and faith. Terry Looper walks with us as a wise, faithful, and surprisingly vulnerable counselor and friend. We long to know God's will for decisions big and small. Terry teaches us how to slow down so that we can truly 'get neutral' enough to discern the voice of God's Spirit in the hubbub of our busy lives. I recommend *Sacred Pace* not only to entrepreneurs and other business leaders, but to all who seek to know God and His will more deeply, so as to live more fully and joyfully."

—MARK ROBERTS, FULLER THEOLOGICAL SEMINARY, EXECUTIVE DIRECTOR OF MAX DE PREE CENTER FOR LEADERSHIP

"*Sacred Pace* is a compelling journey with a powerful spiritual message for everyone—from business leaders to homemakers to young people just starting to find their way in life. It's an engaging read, and I enjoyed every minute of it!"

—SQUIRE RUSHNELL, BESTSELLING AUTHOR OF THE GODWINK SERIES

"I am completely blown away by this book! To write on knowing the will of God is one thing, but to do so in a fresh, unexpected way is truly a Herculean task. *Sacred Pace* is eminently practical, yet at the same time clearly rooted in the Word of God—a balance that is increasingly difficult to find. Another element of this book I find so refreshing is Terry's willingness to talk not only about his successes, but also his failures. This is a wonderful tool for anyone seeking to hear from God and obey His voice."

—DWIGHT EDWARD, PASTOR, WATERGATE COMMUNITY CHURCH

"*Sacred Pace* will not only lead readers toward better results in their decision-making, but also toward a deeper experience in their spiritual lives. I can't think of a combination better than that!"

—ROGER WERNETTE, EXECUTIVE DIRECTOR, THE GATHERING OF MEN

"Reading Terry's story will cause you to reflect on your own story in deep and meaningful ways. The principles in this book are God ordained, and this story must be told!"

—BILL BLOCKER, PRESIDENT, COLLEGE OF BIBLICAL STUDIES

SACRED PACE

SACRED PACE

4 STEPS TO HEARING GOD
AND ALIGNING YOURSELF
WITH HIS WILL

TERRY LOOPER

WITH KRIS BEARSS

W PUBLISHING GROUP

AN IMPRINT OF THOMAS NELSON

Published in Nashville, Tennessee, by W Publishing, an imprint of Thomas Nelson.

Published in association with Yates & Yates, www.yates2.com.

In some cases, names and identifying details in this manuscript have been changed to protect people's privacy.

Thomas Nelson titles may be purchased in bulk for educational, business, fund-raising, or sales promotional use. For information, please e-mail SpecialMarkets@ThomasNelson.com.

ISBN 978-0-7852-2338-2 (eBook)

Library of Congress Control Number: 2018954918

ISBN 978-0-7852-2337-5

Printed in the United States of America

19 20 21 22 23 LSC 10 9 8 7 6 5 4 3 2 1

To Dr. Norman Lawson, who was God's first earthly instrument in liberating my soul and introducing me to the concept of seeking answers from my gut.

CONTENTS

Part 3: Lessons Learned Along the Way

Part 4: Reaching a Sacred Pace in Real Life

FOREWORD

By James Watt, former US Secretary of the Interior

T ERRY LOOPER MAY BE the most successful businessperson you've never heard of. Among his achievements:

- By his midthirties, he had already surpassed his financial dreams.
- At the leading of the Lord, and at great risk after a terrifying personal crisis, he started a niche energy-commodities marketing company with a determination to do two things differently: he would hold to a forty-hour workweek, and he would emphasize customer service over numbers by setting no sales goals. Both approaches are still in place today, thirty years later.
- That company, Texon, has been one of Houston's top five private revenue producers, an industry leader in customer retention, and was selected as a "best place to work" by the *Houston Chronicle*.
- Terry was named an Ernst & Young Gulf Coast Region Entrepreneur of the Year in 2012.
- He gives away 50 percent of everything he makes and has been doing so since 1998.
- He is a devoted Christian, mentor, and family man.
- He is as humble and unselfish as anyone I've ever known.

When I first heard of Terry, I was told in terms both clear and concise: "Do not suggest any fee for your services. Terry Looper is the most generous man you will ever meet." The words came from my friend of many years, Don Hodel, who had served President Reagan as secretary of energy and then succeeded me as secretary of the interior. Since that introduction to Terry about twenty-five years ago, I have watched in amazement as this entrepreneurial capitalist built his company from scratch, being more generous with employees and customers than I or any typical businessman could understand.

In one memorable event, I worked with one of Terry's vice presidents, who had made a fabulous deal with a major oil and gas company. This was a win for the oil company, and it would also yield a significant profit for Texon. Terry decided, though, that Texon was making too much on the deal and insisted the VP rewrite the agreement for the benefit of the oil company.

On a separate occasion, Terry was selling an entire division of Texon to a public company. However, Texon's largest and longest-term customer did not want Terry to sell their portion of the business because the sale would make their primary competitor a key vendor of theirs. Terry heard their management team's concerns, prayerfully weighed all the factors—and exempted their portion from the deal. Texon's entire management team and board thought it was a particularly unwise decision. But because Terry had slowed down and taken the time to work through his four-step decision-making process (the same process you'll learn throughout this book), he was determined not to force people to do what they did not want to do. With God's blessing, that exempted slice of the business ultimately grew to be as big and as profitable a division as the entire business Texon sold to the public company.

These seemingly improbable successes happen all the time in Terry's world because he has learned how to listen not only to people's needs and concerns, but also to the Lord's leading. Using a method

God guided him toward many years ago, Terry carefully sifts through the varying options and opinions in a situation to discern what God wants him to do.

I've seen this process at work again and again from the front row of Terry's life. He doesn't hurry into a decision—he wrestles with it in prayer, a reliance on Scripture, and a rugged weeding-out of whatever earthly influences might be trying to sway him (including his own desires). He will put off giving an answer until he has peace with God on the matter at hand. It is vital to him to have clarity from the Lord before activating a plan, either at home or at work. And yet, somehow, he still makes decisions in a timely manner.

Over the years, those of us on Texon's advisory board have met on a regular basis with Terry and his wife, Doris, to give counsel and advice. Terry, however, would tell you that God is the actual CEO of Texon and that Terry's job is to serve as COO. He fulfills that role so well that as Don and I have headed for the airport after an advisory board meeting, we've frequently shaken our heads in amazement at how Terry, guided by obedience to the leading of the Holy Spirit, could grow and morph the company to nearly unparalleled success by simply seeking God's pace, God's direction, and God's approval before proceeding with a plan.

For starters, Texon regularly earns millions of dollars in revenue while maintaining that founding commitment to a forty-hour workweek and no sales goals. For twenty-nine years running, the company has earned a profit amid often-erratic economic turns, has carried no asset debt, and has never been sued by any of its customers, partners, vendors, or employees. In such a volatile industry, these are remarkable results.

I've frequently expressed my concern to Don that Terry was overpaying the men and women he hired. Terry has always disagreed, but we've never challenged him because his results remain phenomenal. Meanwhile, he and Doris have continued to faithfully give 50 percent of their income to ministries and organizations. Terry also invests untold hours each month mentoring and discipling others in their lives and work.

Truly, Terry's approach to seeking the Lord's will is unlike anything I've ever encountered. Not just because of his success, but because of the peace he's displayed during sometimes enormous challenges and pressing, high-stakes decisions. Terry's process has produced similar results for others, too, easing the anxiety of their decision-making as they allow God to intimately guide their steps.

And now, Terry is sharing his process, as well as his mistakes and some of his story, in these pages.

You may never have the chance to meet Terry Looper in person, but with this book you will have access to his secret to success in business and in life. This most unusual man has something important to say. I hope you'll give him your time. The few hours you'll spend reading *Sacred Pace* could literally change your life.

INTRODUCTION

THIRTY-FIVE YEARS AGO, MY life in the fast lane came to a screeching halt. Everything I thought I knew about who I was and what mattered most came crashing down around me. That season was the worst thing I'd ever experienced—and the best thing that could have happened for my future.

As I began to put the pieces of my life back together, I finally acknowledged that God was in control, not me. And I worked to submit myself to His will in all things.

Because of my newfound desire to know and follow God's will, I began to practice a series of disciplines that allowed me to slow down my way of doing things so I could hear God's voice and obey. As the decades have passed, those disciplines have solidified into a four-step process I refer to as a "sacred pace." Essentially, the four steps help me to wait on God for both His timing and His will in my decisions.

I'm thankful to say the results have been better than I could have imagined, not only for myself spiritually, but for my family, my relationships, and my work as an entrepreneur and CEO in a fiercely competitive, high-stakes industry. Now I'm thirty-five years past that life-altering crisis, with almost as many years practicing this spiritual slowing-down process, and I can confidently say three things:

1. Working through the four steps first, *before* I act on any meaningful decision at home or at work, has become my pathway to receiving clarity and complete peace from the Lord.

2. The concepts behind this sacred pace are grounded in biblical principles, proven spiritual-formation methods, and practical skills that anyone can learn.

3. In three decades of using this approach in everything from the boardroom to intense negotiations to my closest relationships, I have *never* been disappointed by the outcome. Not once.

You Can Find That Pace

My motivation for writing this book isn't complicated: I simply want to help you move forward at God's direction if you're facing a tough decision and you're unsure whether to turn right or left.

Maybe you're on a career fast track yourself and being asked to come up with policies or solutions that affect both the bottom line and other people—and you want the assurance of having chosen wisely. Perhaps you're an exhausted mom or a harried student who struggles to slow down and "be still" (Ps. 46:10), and yet you long to hear from God about His priorities for your busy schedule. Maybe you are single, but you've met someone new and are wondering if this person is God's choice for you. Or perhaps you're married, and you and your spouse are in the midst of a crisis that you just can't see any way through. You might even be a pastor or a worship leader contemplating leaving the ministry.

Whatever decision you're facing, there is a practical, tangible way for you to join pace with God to discover His will and obtain His specific direction. Other people have their methods of discerning what the Lord wants them to do. The four steps you'll read about in this book are mine, and I'm eager to share them with you.

A Personal Decision

If you're skeptical about this process but still curious enough to explore its possibilities, then do what I did: test it and see. Learn the steps, take in the stories from those of us who are regularly trying to practice a different pace, heed our mistakes, and then slow down and apply what you've learned in one situation of your own, regarding one decision. If you're a Christian—someone who has accepted Christ as your Savior—you have His Holy Spirit within you to help you and the Word of God to further guide you.

That's one thing I'm most excited about: *any* follower of Christ can learn to reach this sacred pace where the voice of God can be most clearly heard.

PART I

MY JOURNEY TO
THAT SACRED PACE

CHAPTER 1

COLLISION COURSE

I WAS THIRTY-SIX YEARS old and about to make more money than I'd ever dreamed. Still, I'd never felt more hopeless, more desperate, or more bankrupt.

My situation had been three years in the making—three years of nonstop work, meetings, and cross-country travel, all in pursuit of the glorious dollar. Yet my culminating moment of crisis was so startling that, on this frightening day in the fall of 1984, I couldn't move. Physically, I suppose I could have. *Maybe.* But mentally and emotionally? I was immobilized.

What I was dealing with, no fortune could fix. And for possibly the only time in my life to that point, the dollars didn't matter. They weren't even part of the equation. Suddenly, I wanted to be *well*, not wealthy.

In this terrifying turn of events, I would've given every penny that was coming to me if only I could have myself back.

Working My Plan

I'd prepared myself for business success my entire life. At age six, I aspired to own a men's clothing store because the man who ran the one in my little Texas town was the only entrepreneur I knew. Through high school, I racked up a full list of extracurricular activities.

First and foremost, I got involved in almost every service organization and school club possible—and sought to be a leader in each of them. I became president of my class, vice president of the student body, treasurer of the Key Club, and was a regular at church, among a lot of other activities. But one issue always hindered me when it came to my choices: I was an extreme people pleaser.

In situation after situation, group after group, I wanted the accomplishment but never the heat. For example, I turned down the chance to be Key Club president because it might mean making decisions that would offend people. Being class president didn't really involve any controversy; it was mostly a social position, so I was safe there. And of course, being vice president of anything meant the president was calling the real shots.

This was an insecurity I took with me into college and beyond.

When I went to Lamar University, I chose my major—and even predetermined my graduating grade point average—at the advice of my neighbor, an oil refinery plant manager who probably had the biggest job in my hometown of Texas City, Texas. He told me, "Study engineering; there's good money in that. And make at least a 3.0 grade point average so you can stand out."

And so I did.

When it came to grades, I was capable of better—I had nearly perfect math scores on my pre-college SATs—but in my mind, to do anything more academically was a waste of time. Why read an entire book when I could find summaries in the library and make "good enough" grades?

School was just a means to an end. The activities were my focus—serving as vice president of my fraternity and student president of the engineering department, and running a coin-operated foosball-table business in fraternity houses and beer joints for extra income. As my final semester of college approached, I knew what grades I needed for a 3.0, so I decided ahead of time that I would make two As and two Bs—just enough to reach the goal. And sure enough, I graduated with a 3.01.

During those four years I did a lot of notable things, the best of which was marrying my high school sweetheart, Doris, my junior year. But I never did feel at peace about me. I was always in a hurry to get somewhere and impress somebody, though I couldn't say where or who. Nevertheless, I believed that my future in business was bright and that my greatest successes were just around the corner.

Driving Hard and Fast

My first job after college was as a maintenance foreman at the agrochemical giant Monsanto. It wasn't my first choice—I really wanted a sales job—but when none was offered, I went back to Texas City where I knew people. Within two years, after working my way up from maintenance to pollution engineer, Monsanto transferred me to sales.

For the first six months or so of sales training, they didn't want me selling anything; I was just supposed to watch, listen, and learn from their team. This was very frustrating for me because I was interested in "doing." With a wife and a baby girl, Tanya, at home, I wanted to be let loose so I could start making big money. My boss, though, kept putting on the brakes. He went so far as to specifically tell an overly eager me, "Just continue your training, Terry; no selling for now."

In my zeal, however, I rushed ahead and didn't listen. I'm fortunate I didn't get fired, because I actually set up a client meeting, drove to the big city (Houston), and took a blank contract with me, hoping to snag my first deal.

The customer was willing to sign. I was so excited!

When I asked for the official name of his company for the paperwork, the man answered, "Dresser, Inc."

My embarrassing reply? "I didn't know you were also in the ink business." (Can you tell I never earned an MBA?)

Somehow I managed to recover from that blunder and was successively promoted four times in six years. I loved the marketing and sales work, and evidently it showed, because corporate kept giving me more responsibility. I even grew a mustache on my baby face in order to be taken seriously as a negotiator of deals.

In time, however, my job became so stressful that it affected my health. I mostly suffered from indigestion, which maybe isn't a big deal when you're fifty, but it was pretty significant for me as a twenty-six-year-old. The company awarded me a $2,000 bonus for my work on a successful deal. It was the first bonus I'd ever received. Yet as grateful as I was for the money, it didn't relieve my health issues. Finally, after several months of trying to juggle everything, I reluctantly gave back one of the product lines I was managing—it was just too much for me.

One year later I received a big promotion, and the family and I moved from St. Louis to San Jose, California, where I served as regional manager for petrochemicals. Regional sales were small enough that I also made sales calls. One of my frequent calls was to a super successful entrepreneur out of Las Vegas named Ken. Gravitating toward entrepreneurs as I did, I was in awe of Ken and his lifestyle. He and his colleagues were not only inventors but innovators—the company founder had invented the Styrofoam "clamshell" for burgers that revolutionized fast-food packaging back in the '70s—and they'd all made a fortune. Someday soon, I hoped I could do something revolutionary myself and enjoy the payday that came with it.

Scratching the Itch

My sales roles meant traveling. A lot. Which meant being away from my young family, which had recently expanded with the birth of our daughter Jeannie, for days at a time. I was doing breakfasts, lunches, and dinners with clients, leaving me with nothing but fumes for my wife and kids.

Not surprisingly, Doris and I were struggling. Between my job and my excessive drive to succeed, I was essentially forcing Doris to be a single mom during the week and then expecting her to be an attentive wife on the weekends—never mind that I had very little left for her!

I was putting our marriage in jeopardy, but I was too focused on my pursuit of success to admit it.

A year and a half later, in 1979, I was transferred back to Houston as a manager in Monsanto's biggest petrochemical region. Doris says of me at that time: "Whatever role Terry was in, he was always looking at what hat he would wear next."

That's true. And now that I'd experienced the corporate world, the hat I most wanted to try was that of entrepreneur. My childhood itch for having my own company had never gone away. If anything, the itch was getting harder to ignore. I yearned for my own thing, not another position buried within the hierarchy of a huge conglomerate.

The secure paycheck had been a blessing in the early years of my career while Doris and I started a family. However, I was well aware that the only way you make money in a Fortune 100 environment such as Monsanto is to climb the ladder. As I looked to the rungs above me, I saw no future: I wanted neither my boss's job, nor his boss's job, nor *his* boss's job! So I resigned and, as a next step, switched to a smaller company. I joined a privately owned, Houston-based refinery, eager for a new challenge and excited to learn the oil business. Unfortunately, three months after I changed jobs, President Reagan decontrolled oil, and the company I was with quickly started bleeding red ink. Heeding the writing on the wall, I kept my ear to the ground for another job, and within several months I was able to join Ken in an energy-marketing company that he was starting.

Ken and I had stayed in touch after I'd left California, and the timing of his business launch was perfect. Most important to me were the opportunities to have unlimited income potential and to be involved from the ground floor. It was like kerosene to my entrepreneurial fire.

Addicted to Success

Our business was a zoo. And Ken was brilliant.

He was also an unbelievably driven man who demanded perfection.

My addiction to success and my lust for money couldn't have been a better match for this startup world. I did deals all day long. When one was done, I was already anticipating the next three or four, absolutely absorbed with the prospects and possibilities of *more*. Like twenty-four-hour talk radio, my mind never turned off. Neither did Ken's. He and I would be on the phone at least an hour every day (on landlines, no less!), sometimes late into the night, no matter what time zone either of us was in.

All our overtime hours helped the company grow rapidly. With four regional offices, money was rolling in fast. Ken eventually awarded me a 10 percent share in the company and designated me second-in-command. His office was in Vegas, and I was in Houston; between us, we ran it all.

To keep up with the excessive demands of our increasing client base and manage our entire staff of more than 150 employees nationwide, I had to be constantly on the go. Yet there was more to my frenzy than "keeping up"; I was also trying to make my relentless business partner happy—and fuel my own need to be noticed.

The pace was wearing me out. Even worse, my neglect of my wife and daughters was becoming a way of life. Each night during the workweek, Doris would prepare my dinner on a mustard-colored plate, along with dinner for her and the girls, and then set it aside for whenever I got home. Most nights, my dining room chair remained empty until long after their dinner was done.

I was absent so much that when my eldest, Tanya, would check the stands at her grade-school gymnastics meets, the question in her mind was always: *Is Dad here? Did he make it?* She never doubted whether she'd see her mom or her younger sister, Jeannie. But too often I was barely on time, if I made it at all.

I missed out on a lot during those years. My family, though, paid the biggest price, enduring broken promises, scrapped plans, and a lot of disappointment while I chased down the next dollar. Sometimes it was smaller neglects, such as promising Doris or the girls early in the week, "We'll go to a movie on Saturday," and then being too exhausted to follow through on the weekend. But I also ignored my family's needs in much bigger ways, such as when our seven-year-old, Jeannie, kept asking me to help with her math homework, which was my specialty. Rather than giving her my time, which is what she really wanted, I opted for a more "convenient" solution that would let me stay focused on my plans: "I'll hire you a tutor, honey." (Naturally, she declined.)

Another time, about thirteen years into our marriage, Doris had major surgery, and I actually told her, "I'll come with you to the hospital, but I will have to leave later and let your mom take care of you. There's a cocktail party scheduled, and lots of industry people will be there."

Things between Doris and me had been strained for a long time, to say the least. In my obsession with work, I denied what I was doing to us and blamed her for our problems. In truth, no matter what she tried, I didn't please easily. She would buy me clothes (I don't know how many pairs of blue jeans she picked out for me), but none of them were ever quite right. Instead of affirming everything she did to keep our home a loving, organized, life-giving place, I would pressure her—"Join the Junior League; get out of the house and volunteer"—because I thought that was the image we needed to have.

It was so unfair. Doris was focused on what really mattered—being a remarkable parent to our girls, serving as taxi driver and disciplinarian and helper as our daughters needed in my absences—and I wanted her attending swanky luncheons and hobnobbing with Houston's elite.

She admits now that she never felt good enough in those days. What woman would, with a husband who treated her as I did?

It wasn't only her, though; I was never satisfied with anything. Not the car I drove, or the deals I made, or the nice house we owned. No matter how good things got, no matter how well I or anyone else did, it was never enough—never good enough—in my eyes.

My perspective was so messed up that one time, before leaving on a business trip, I told Doris over lunch, "I'm not sure I love you anymore."

She shot back, "Yes, you do; you're just confused."

"It was a God thing that I stayed," she says now. "My role was being a mother to our precious girls and providing as happy of a home for them as I could—and that included staying married to Terry."

Running Scared

I understand now that at the root of my perpetual discontentment was the perpetual fear that *I* wasn't good enough; that no one—my parents, my business partner, my wife or daughters or anyone else—could ever accept me unless I kept achieving and accumulating. I was essentially running scared, trying to outdo whatever I'd done the day before in hopes of silencing, once and for all, the insecurities that had been driving my decisions since childhood. Yet each day was the same as the one before: somebody would be upset or another deal awaited or there was money to be made—and somehow, the *more* I was so fanatically pursuing was never sufficient. Around and around I went, ever circling but never reaching a place where I could catch my breath and freely enjoy the view. Instead, I drove myself harder and justified my absences and nonstop activity as righteous sacrifices backed by the best of intentions.

The millions I'll make will provide every material thing my family could want. That was how I consoled myself. Deep down, though, I was a people-pleasing, money-chasing little boy—and no amount of cash or accomplishment was going to change that.

I had entered myself in an impossible race I couldn't win. A race with no finish line and no water breaks. The only break I ever took was on Sunday mornings, when I would pause long enough to attend Bible class and church with my family. I did this every week. This wasn't a matter of heartfelt commitment; it was more of the same old thing: more about appearances and trying to gain favor with God (and maybe with my wife too). Deep inside, I was telling myself, *See? I'm a good man! And a good Christian.* And that's what I wanted everyone else to think. But as soon as church was done, I was back to the real me—the me that couldn't stay off the gerbil wheel.

I just wouldn't stop. I'd envisioned being an entrepreneur for far too long. What's more, I had forfeited my career track at Monsanto for this chance. I figured, *The hours are simply the price you pay to be in business.*

My "Crazy Days"

As I went faster and faster on this track with no restraint whatsoever, Doris saw me deteriorating before her eyes. She remembers that during my "crazy days," the pink phone slips we used were constantly falling out of my pockets—reminders of calls I needed to make and people I needed to see. Even so, Doris was helpless to stop the madness because I wouldn't admit the extreme pressure I was feeling. Given my mindset at the time, to admit anything like that would have amounted to a betrayal of my dreams.

Rather than change the way I was operating, I drank martinis for lunch and again before I came home from work, and then I kept taking calls and meetings late into the evening. The success and the lure of money were just too intoxicating for me to resist. No one, however, can keep up this pace forever. And sometime during year two of the startup, I began feeling dizzy. The sensation would come and go, but some days it lingered long enough that I'd have to close my office door and lie down on the floor until I felt better.

As time went on, my symptoms grew worse. Where once I could effortlessly strategize and run numbers in my mind to determine the best deal, now I was barely getting through some of my meetings because I *just couldn't make decisions.* I was making more and more mistakes as well: I hired a vice president but forgot to tell his subordinates before he arrived. I got on the wrong plane two different times. We built a small refinery in Nevada without initially submitting any permits. Ken and I flew together on one trip and put on each other's suit coat as we were exiting the plane, only to be rescued from our mistake by an observant flight attendant.

You get the picture.

Feeling very unlike myself, but with no idea of what was happening to me, I went to a doctor, and he attributed my bouts of dizziness to stress.

"Can you give me a pill?" I asked, hoping for a quick fix. "I need something for this."

"Sorry, Mr. Looper," he said. "I'm not giving you anything."

All the other doctors hand out pills! I thought. But shocked as I was, this physician held his ground, perhaps accurately diagnosing that my symptoms were not a sickness; my priorities were the real problem.

Trouble Ahead

Without any medication to ease my pain, I continued to spiral physically and mentally. Over the next year, not only did my dizziness worsen, but my brain fogged to the point that I struggled to make routine decisions such as where to eat lunch. Still, the symptoms weren't enough to sideline me. I just kept pushing to my limit. After all, time was on my side—I was still young. Surely I could sustain the workload until our company really made it big.

When Ken decided to sell the company to a public utility at the end of our third year, my pride and insecurity did not want to let it go. But my body was ready. More ready than I imagined.

Little did I know I was about to hit the proverbial wall that marathoners speak of—that point where your muscles and lungs are sizzling with the burn of lactic acid and your reserves are depleted but without the runner's high that follows it.

And it would nearly destroy me.

CHAPTER 2

THE CRASH

I HIT THAT WALL one life-altering Saturday at our home in Houston, a couple of months after Ken's decision to sell the company.

After ignoring month upon month of warning signs, I suddenly could not get out of bed. It felt like the oxygen had been turned off in my brain, making it impossible for me to even lift my head from the pillow.

This was more than just a physical sensation. It was emotional, spiritual, and mental. A shutdown on every level. My predominant feeling was that my brain had quit—just like that—and I was having a nervous breakdown. My brain had stopped so abruptly, it was as if someone had thrown a rock into my gears.

Fear and dread taunted me: what if this was permanent? What if I hadn't simply run out of gas but had pushed myself to the point that my internal machinery had *worn out*, with no hope of repair? I was terrified what that might mean for me and my family. And yet, I had no one to blame but myself. I had insisted on speeding ahead on my own power, completely ignoring the brake pedal. I was intent on doing things *my way*, listening only to me, living like I knew best, exceeding every limit. And I had. Now I couldn't do anything for myself.

I truly thought I had lost my mind at age thirty-six. Worst of all, I wasn't sure I would ever get it back.

At What Cost?

If the last rule of competition is, "You cannot quit until you cannot walk at all," I had held to it. But at what cost? Emotions frayed, mind completely fried, I insisted that Doris keep our bedroom door closed and the curtains shut so I could be covered in darkness.

A frantic Doris called my sister to come over on that fateful Saturday, and they talked through whether to proceed with the next day's plans, when I was scheduled to be ordained as an elder at our church. They also discussed what no wife ever imagines when she vows "in sickness and in health": which mental-health facility to put me in.

Later that morning, after some hours of undisturbed rest, I somehow managed to crawl onto my knees, more scared than I'd ever been, and cry, "Lord, I can't go on like this. I've done a miserable job of trying to run my life by myself. You need to take control, because I've screwed everything up."

They were the only words I had in me.

On that day, I reached out to the God I knew, though I—a guy who was less than twenty-four hours from being installed in a leadership position in my church—barely knew Him at all.

Having grown up in church, I'd never doubted that He was Creator and Ruler of the universe; I just hadn't wanted Him to be *my* God because I had a god already: money. I was much like the rich young ruler in Mark 10 who said, "Jesus, I've followed Your commandments my whole life—never murdered anybody, or stolen from anyone, or defrauded anybody" (vv. 19–20, my paraphrase), but who was unwilling to become a real disciple because, as author and pastor John Piper described it, his "fist [was] clenched around his wealth."[1]

There was no denying, though, that my way of doing things had failed. Now that I'd caught my money-god and courted my mistresses—acceptance, people pleasing, achievement—I found myself facedown on the floor of my blacked-out bedroom, taunted by the harsh reality that I'd stood my ladder of success against the wrong wall, and that wall had collapsed. I'd made a wreck of my life. A complete crash and burn.

It was the worst day I'd ever known.

The Aftermath

That worst of days was excruciating for a classic overachiever like me. I'd accomplished almost everything I'd ever set my mind to—not by brilliance, but by determination and a country boy's ingenuity and a knack for sales. That is, until my overloaded neurons short-circuited. Then everything slammed to a halt and went blank, and I was brought to my knees.

Thankfully, after my anguished prayer that Saturday in October, my brain did flicker on again. But it was only a flicker. For my ordination service the next morning, Doris and my sister had to choose my clothes for me and then escort me to my seat in the church sanctuary. That's how debilitated I was.

Still unsure of what had happened, I took a week off work to regain some equilibrium. I also visited a psychologist, who gave me a book on burnout. When I read that, I learned two things: 1) I had indeed burned out, and 2) it would happen again if I didn't change my ways and do some serious therapy.

A few weeks later, when the time came to fly to Vegas to sign the company sale documents, I was still so disoriented that I admitted to my sister, "I think I'm too dizzy to fly." She offered to go with me, "because you have given your life for this."

Indeed I had.

Still Disappointed

Once the papers were signed, I should've been on top of the world: I was not just a millionaire as I'd always hoped, but a *multi*millionaire! Yet the money didn't remove the hollowness inside.

For one, I still didn't feel noticed by my parents. My mother, especially, was a tough one to impress. A math whiz who won state competitions every year throughout high school in algebra and geometry, she was so gifted that she no doubt would have thrived in college. Unfortunately, her family didn't have the money for her to attend. And with her being a woman in an earlier era, she was expected to get married and have children, not further her education.

After marrying my dad, she got a job as assistant to the president for an oil company, and hers was the approval I sought most. Since I never could earn it with my activities or accomplishments, I tried with dollars. Though when I called to share this huge career milestone with her, instead of celebrating me, Mother's response was, "But you ruined your health."

I couldn't argue with her. Nevertheless, her words felt like a punch to the gut.

Clearly, my issues ran deep. I needed far more help than anyone around me knew how to give. So Doris and my sister found a therapist in the Yellow Pages who, providentially, turned out to be a man of strong faith and an expert at ushering people through their deepest insecurities. And as soon as the sale of the business closed in November, I started therapy. Intense, deep therapy, twice a week. I didn't care what it took; I wasn't going to lose my mind again.

I told this man, "I'll do as much work as I need to." (Being scared out of your mind has a way of changing your mind, doesn't it?)

He indicated it would take a lot of time to unpack my pain.

He wasn't kidding.

Rebuild

The utility that bought our company retained me as COO of this new division and gave me oversight of all commercial accounts across three divisions. Neither Ken nor I had wanted to be CEO, so the utility selected someone who had been an executive in one of their regulated divisions. As you can imagine, for this guy, whom I'll call Bill, to be named president of such an extremely entrepreneurial group as ours was not a seamless fit.

Neither was my role an entrepreneur's dream—it felt more like a wilderness to me. When I wanted to fire the vice president of one of the divisions, Bill said, "No, we're not firing him. I like him." I responded by offering to demote myself: "Then let me run only one division. You can have the other two, and that guy can report to you."

Bill took me up on it, which worked out well on one hand because it allowed me to concentrate on the hard-core emotional and spiritual realignment that was already underway in my life. I'd totaled things so completely that every part of me needed to be overhauled. The good news is, it happened. Slowly but surely.

I guess you could say that in those post-burnout years, my life underwent a rebuild from the wheels up. While I was "in the shop," God was retooling me with a different operating system—a different way of thinking and working. He reset my priorities altogether and helped me settle into a new pace that He promised would cause much less wear and tear than my fast-track pursuits had. I found that guarantee in the Bible where Jesus told His listeners, "Take my yoke upon you. Let me teach you, because I am humble and gentle at heart, and you will find rest for your souls. For my yoke is easy to bear, and the burden I give you is light" (Matt. 11:29–30, NLT).

Particularly for the first year or so, with my foot off the gas pedal at home and at work, everything felt like an experiment because I was trying to unlearn lifelong patterns and develop new ones. It was a laboratory for the soul. Fortunately, I found that as long as I stayed within the parameters that are in every Christian's owner's manual (the Bible), my life not only ran more effectively, but I started seeing the kinds of results—relationally and spiritually—I'd been seeking my entire life. I was becoming less impulsive in my decision-making. Less distracted by dollar signs. And definitely braver in the face of my fears, especially my fear of displeasing others. Plus, I felt better.

Others saw a difference, too, first and foremost Doris and my daughters. But then also my friends, and eventually my colleagues.

Probably what surprised me most during this tentative time was how much I grew to love Scripture. The Word of God was undeniably recalibrating my heart and mind, breathing life into my soul. For the first time ever, I felt excited to open my Bible each day; it was speaking to me in profoundly practical ways I hadn't noticed before. I marveled at this newfound spiritual hunger, and I gave therapy all the credit. Then one day Doris remarked that God had really changed my heart, and I finally put two and two together: therapy wasn't the only reason my life was different. Jesus had clearly done a work inside me as well.

With the mental fog lifted, I could now see that Saturday a year ago was a turning point. My day of salvation. When I had gasped that genuine, pleading prayer at the bottom of my burnout, I was born again; I simply hadn't realized it. For an entire year, I didn't know!

This has puzzled some people. "How could you not know, Terry?" they ask. "The moment of salvation is usually as obvious as a lit-up fire truck coming at you with its sirens on!" All I can say is, my slow discovery shows the extent of my spiritual blindness and denial.

I was so "accomplished" at religious activities that I assumed I'd been a Christian for most of my life. I mean, with my résumé, how could I not be? I looked the part through and through! Weekly church attender since childhood. Regular tither. Even church elder. What I lacked, though, was the kind of transformation that only Christ can produce: a change of heart from the inside out.

Once I surrendered to Him as the only One who could rescue me from myself, I began the lengthy process of shedding my well-worn "cultural Christianity" and living in the reality and security of my new identity. I was a child of God—forgiven, loved, accepted.

As this sunk in, my perspective slowly changed, and then, so did my patterns. Jesus was no longer a convenience; He became a deep consideration and my Friend—someone I looked to for counsel and could be completely transparent with about my insecurities. I quit compartmentalizing Him as a "for Sundays only" entity and actually started engaging with Him day after day, *wanting* to know Him, eagerly studying His life and words, interested in what He thought about the things I was facing.

My therapist reinforced my spiritual zeal by introducing me to the writings of Christians past and present who had dedicated their lives to heeding Christ's instruction in His Word (the Bible) and in the ever-present voice of His Spirit in their hearts and minds. As I learned their ways, I tried to put His Word into practice. I tried to slow down and listen for the Holy Spirit's whispers in my day-to-day life. And I was changing.

Family Time and God's Time

The lesser responsibility at work made it possible for me to be as all in with my family as I'd ever dreamed. I was able to have dinner with Doris and the girls practically every night and to do special things for the kids, such as build Tanya a balance beam in our backyard and help Jeannie build a gingerbread house for fun. We also started traveling as a family. It was so much fun! We took a lot of trips during those years and made wonderful memories. Still, I was prone to overdo even good things. God used my family to help rein me in.

One summer day, while in the early stages of some long-term vacation planning, I asked Doris and the girls, "Where do you want to go for Thanksgiving and Christmas this year?" Tanya and Jeannie's response was immediate: "Nowhere. You've worn us out!"

In retrospect, it was another lesson in my "driver's training." Situations like this would teach me to be quicker to hit the brakes for myself next time I started going too fast. More importantly, I was understanding why I needed brakes in the first place.

Whenever something exciting is ahead of me, my inclination—to this day—is to speed up in order to obtain it as quickly as I can, and then to keep adding to my supply. You could say I've always been about acceleration and accumulation.

Therapy has helped me see that a lot of it is my attempt to compensate for what I lacked growing up: not only did I feel unseen by my parents and others, but we simply didn't do much as a family. Vacations, for example, were rare. God continues to teach me, however, that the compulsion to either speed up or add on to the good things He has given me are warning signals. I need to treat them as a dashboard alert: "Time to run a diagnostic, Terry, to see what's really behind your push."

On one family vacation we did take in the summer of 1986 (about a year and a half after the buyout), I came across one of those magazine quizzes titled something like "Are You Ready to Be an Entrepreneur?" Nineteen of my answers corresponded exactly with the traits and mindset of someone who should launch a startup. But the singular question I could not answer in the affirmative was major: *Would you give yourself completely to your company in order to succeed?*

I knew how real this was, the pace an entrepreneur has to sustain. I was simply not willing to forfeit my family and my well-being again. If I was supposed to start my own company, that roadblock would have to be removed for me. For now, though, the roadblock was most definitely there. Nevertheless, the thought of venturing out on my own wouldn't go away. Being in business for myself seemed to be a desire of my heart—it was always what I came back to after exploring other options. Yet I'd proven my desires couldn't be trusted.

Seeing no way to reconcile these competing concerns, I just stayed in my lane and kept praying for God to show me what to do.

Bored and Boxed In

What was a boon for me personally—the oversight of only one small division at work—was a real struggle for me professionally. I got bored pretty fast. My assistant knew something needed to change when she caught me absentmindedly doodling on an unpeeled banana at my desk one day. "Tell me you're not doing that," was her lone comment.

A friend of mine in the company recognized my boredom and prodded me to think bigger: "Why don't you get involved in business development?" I liked that idea, so I went to Bill and asked if he'd let me develop new business for a percentage. "No, that's my job," he said, adding, "You need to stop making suggestions; bosses don't want them unless they ask."

That certainly wasn't the answer I'd hoped for. But it did cause me to think more seriously about a job change, maybe even a career move. My sister wisely advised, "Though you're feeling boxed in, stay employed until you find what's next so that your mind doesn't go idle."

CHAPTER 3

....

A WAY TO HIS WILL

IN THE FALL OF 1986, I had a complete break with Ken. An issue came up and he threatened, "If you don't vote my way, we won't do business anymore." It was an insignificant issue that I couldn't support, so I voted the way I thought best—and never heard from Ken again.

I can see now that his ultimatum was a blessing in disguise, as was Bill's refusal to let me explore new ideas. Their decisions eliminated options for me more quickly than I might have done for myself. Ken's reaction, for example, revealed there was no going back into business with him, and Bill's response effectively shut the door on a career with the utility, for I clearly was not a fit.

Like many new Christians, I did wonder if God might be calling me out of corporate life and into full-time ministry. *Maybe I should be a youth pastor or run a homeless ministry* were frequent considerations throughout the next year and a half. All the while, I couldn't help but speculate about buying or starting a company myself.

One opportunity came up around this time that seemed a perfect combination of safety net and professional synergy. A utility proposed starting a third-party marketing company that would also purchase energy products—a line of business that was right up my alley—and we would be fifty-fifty partners. They would put up all the capital and credit, and I would run the operation. For nine months, we negotiated. I met with the president of the division and the CFO, and they obtained board approval. It seemed like everything was a go until one day, while I was out on the slopes, the president of the utility called and said, "We've decided we can't move forward with you, Terry. You're too entrepreneurial."

I'm thankful now that God worked in my circumstances to keep me on course toward His will. He knew my heart and that I truly wanted His best for me. That meant trusting Him and Him alone as my next Partner, not looking to a financial or corporate partner as my security. That would've been a complete crutch, only I wasn't supposed to have any crutches this time around. I can imagine Him saying, "We're going to dive off the cliff, and you don't get to have a parachute."

Beautiful Things

Between my own career ideas and proposals like these from other businesspeople, the options were many. And they drove me crazy. They also drove me closer to Christ.

It seems the Lord is always slower with His answers than we would like. I believe one reason is He wants us to develop more trust and dependence on Him. That was definitely an area of prayer for me in 1988, even as I yearned to move ahead with whatever God had in store.

I made it my habit to sit quietly at the beginning of each day, prayerfully asking the Lord, "What's next? What is Your plan for me?" I'd then read from my Bible and a devotional before proceeding with my day.

Two beautiful things happened as I waited on the Lord. First, God kept drawing me to a verse within Scripture that spoke very practically to my fear: "Trust in the LORD with all your heart, and lean not on your own understanding; in all your ways acknowledge Him, and He shall direct your paths" (Prov. 3:5–6, NKJV).

I felt very personally heard by the One I'd been praying to all this time—and deeply reassured. It was true that my desires couldn't be trusted if I was concerned with what *I* wanted. But for nearly three years I'd been operating at a slower pace and actively seeking the Lord for my next move, which meant I could rely on the Guide and Helper He had given me at the moment of my salvation, His Holy Spirit, to lead the way.

It was right there in black and white! If I submitted myself to the Lord's wisdom, He would simultaneously direct my steps and ensure that my heart's desires echoed my heavenly Father's desires for me. That was the burst of faith I needed to rest in the Lord until He advised my next move.

The other beautiful thing that happened was that I not only downshifted into a slower gear but actually shifted into "neutral." That's how I thought of it. For the first time ever, I quit insisting on having things my way and moving ahead with my plans. Rather, I became ambitious for God's will, and His alone, whatever that might mean for my future. I now wanted God's will over my preferences and was ready to do whatever He decided. This further shift changed the content of my prayers from "Here's what I want, God, please help me," to "Lord, what do *You* want me to do?" And I truly meant it.

The way I'd been praying prior to getting neutral wasn't wrong. In fact, it was a good starting point. It just wasn't where I ultimately needed to land.

God wants us to come to Him with our specific needs and desires. We see this in the example of the psalmist in Psalm 5:2–3: "Hear my cry for help, my King and my God, for to you I pray. In the morning, LORD, you hear my voice; in the morning I lay my requests before you and wait expectantly." And in the biblical exhortation of verses such as Ephesians 6:18: "Pray in the Spirit on all occasions with all kinds of prayers and requests." But in order to receive God's answers, we must bring *ourselves* to Him as well—"all [our] heart" and "all [our] ways" (Prov. 3:5–6). This includes everything from our emotions and thoughts to our motives and dreams and plans, not just our requests. We must keep bringing our hearts and minds to Him until we are assured that He not only knows better than we do, but He knows best. From this place of trust and willing obedience, we are lovingly beckoned forward, toward the blessings the Lord has planned for us.

As I prayerfully weighed everything that had happened since my burnout alongside the things God had been teaching me, the arrows all seemed to point in one direction: toward starting my own company. Once that part of the equation bubbled up, I had a peace that wasn't ever there before. I recalled reading in the Bible that the movement of God is marked by a peace that "transcends all understanding" (Phil. 4:7). The dots were connecting in a wonderful way.

Now the question became, Was I going to wait for the rest of His answer—the when and the how—or just start any old business? Encouraged by the partial answer, and especially by the deep peace that accompanied it, I resolved to wait. Meanwhile, I would continue doing what God had shown me to do thus far. I would keep praying and paying attention to the direction of His Spirit in my life, mind, and heart.

From then on, whenever a business possibility came to mind, I'd intentionally slow down, seek what Jesus wanted me to know, and continually wrestle with my will until I longed for His best above anything else. Once I got neutral, I tried to stay "parked" and listen until I had full peace about an answer. Confusion or uncertainty meant *wait longer*. No peace meant the answer was no. Only when I was given a yes with peace would I inch ahead.

Forging a Future

In hindsight, the Holy Spirit was continuing the work He'd begun inside me after my burnout. Back in the early days of therapy, I had vowed that I would give Jesus full say in whatever I did going forward.

He would be not just my Lord and Savior in life, but my Business Partner in any future ventures.

I viewed this possibility of starting my own company as a chance to test out my faith and see how it worked in real-world conditions. If I acknowledged the Lord, including Him and consulting Him at every turn in this critical decision, I had His word: He would show me the way. In my simple thinking that meant, *If I let Him map my route and set my speed, I can just follow His directions.*

A key circumstance occurred in the fall of 1988, when Don Hodel—the secretary of the interior under President Reagan—gave his testimony at our church. I later dreamed up a crazy idea: *what if Secretary Hodel would join my new company?* After Reagan and his cabinet left office early the following year, I was able to arrange a meeting and fly to Colorado to discuss my proposal with Don and his wife, Barbara.

After a day of trailing Don on the blue runs of the slopes of Keystone, I had my chance. The three of us met in a hotel lobby to discuss the possibility of him joining my company. As we were wrapping up, he said, "We should pray about this."

"By all means, you and Barbara should pray," I replied.

He chuckled. "I meant all of us, right now. In this lobby."

This was the first time I had ever prayed with someone I was negotiating with, much less in the most public space of a hotel.

To my great surprise, Don later agreed to join the company. It felt like a huge confirmation of the Lord's hand in this decision, because I never imagined that I'd even get to meet with a former presidential cabinet member, much less hire one. Still, I was undoubtedly missing the final, complex piece of the puzzle. It was my three-dimensional deal breaker, my nonnegotiable: how could I honor my family, be successful, and avoid burning out—all at the same time? From my perspective, accomplishing two of these priorities was doable, but all three? Impossible.

It was a perplexing dilemma. I'd messed up my family and my health so much that if starting a company meant going back to who I'd been and how I'd lived before, I didn't want any part of it. I had developed a new relationship with my wife and daughters that was better than anything before, and I had a relationship with the Lord I'd never imagined could happen. I even had Don Hodel in my back pocket. Yet I had no solution whatsoever for bringing all these facts and circumstances, priorities and passions together.

What I also had, for the first time ever, was absolute conviction. I'd always felt I had morals, but not until I became a Christian did I start having convictions. I was so convinced that "family and no burnout" was God's priority that I couldn't deviate from it. But I also deeply wanted to succeed in my work.

All I could do was keep praying that God would give me an answer if He wanted me to go forward. And if He didn't want me going forward with this prospect, I prayed He would redirect me elsewhere.

Doing Differently

The answer started to unfold further thanks to a compelling audio-cassette titled *Why Go to Work?* (which has since been published as a booklet by the same title).[1] Its scripturally based message—part of a series produced by a business ministry—was so counterintuitive that I listened to it repeatedly, trying to absorb this fresh line of thought.

The essence was that while God commands us to work hard while we work, He also instituted regular, rhythmic periods of rest. (For example: day and night, planting season and harvest time, the Sabbath, and so on). Both our labor and our rest allow us unique opportunities to serve God with our time, furthering His purposes and His kingdom in different ways. Both are also meant to reflect our dependence on Him for our security rather than self-reliance.

Limiting how much we work, and being obedient to the times of rest He has ordained, reminds us that it is God who ultimately provides for our needs.

Obviously, these were truths I needed to integrate into my life. One example from the tape really hit home. The speaker talked about the two typical ways that people approach business planning. Quoting from the booklet (since the tape is no longer available):

> [Planning] is done according to *priorities* or according to *income*. In the latter the planner determines beforehand how much he wants to make in the year and then orders his priorities accordingly. In the former he determines before God his priorities, and on that basis how many hours God wants him to spend in his vocation each week. . . .
>
> If . . . he plans according to income, he will allow the marketplace to dictate the level of his commitment to Jesus Christ. When he perceives that his needs are not being properly met and that he is not reaching his financial goals, he will begin to work harder instead of looking to God. Family priorities, time with the Lord, and ministry commitments will give way to the pressing need of meeting financial goals.[2]

My previous way of thinking was reflected in every aspect of the message. Between my burnout and the way I'd strained my family relationships in the pursuit of money, there was no question about it: I'd been that guy who had let the marketplace dictate all my commitments. Every priority I should have had was treated more like a hobby ("as I had time").

In my burnout, such chasing after the wind had lost its appeal. I had the Lord and His Word guiding me, I had done therapy, and I'd seen the transformation in my family life. The courage and the intention to operate according to a new paradigm were in place. Now all I needed was clarity, especially if I was going into business for myself. Until I had that, I would keep waiting.

The Final Pieces

I'm certainly no saint. My "patience" was nothing other than a divinely motivated refusal to go backward and make the same mistakes. But the Lord helped me stand firm while I waited, and soon an idea started to form. It pieced together all that I was learning, in addition to what I'd been praying for and talking through with others since my burnout. It also accounted for the realities and circumstances that were before me in this specific situation. Most surprisingly, it incorporated the longings of my heart. The idea was this: *I'd like to start a company that would duplicate what Ken and I did [servicing the oil and gas industry] but that in no way duplicates the way we did it.*

The more I prayed about it, the more my heart was stirred. And what began as an idea soon became a conviction that seemed motivated by the Lord: any company of mine would either have to do business far differently than I'd seen and done in my past (though the "how" and "if" were still to be determined), or else there would be no company. I was neutral about God's answer—He would decide what was best, company or no company. Either way, I was okay with it.

Early in 1989, the Lord took my neutral mindset one critical step further, but in a very non-Terry direction. *What if I worked only forty hours per week and had no sales goals?*

I was terrified. And intrigued.

On one hand, it just might work. It could also fail miserably. The businessman in me kept thinking, *How silly is this idea? Is this really of the Lord?* Even if it was, I wondered if I would actually follow through on trusting His ways over mine. To do this would mean I was putting up 100 percent of the capital required; if I was wrong about any of it, Doris and I could lose our entire retirement nest egg. Yet if this approach was from God, I certainly didn't want to miss it.

To my spiritual heart, it made perfect sense. To my entrepreneur's mind, though, it was just plain ludicrous. Three realities counterbalanced my doubts.

First, it was such an out-of-the-box solution that I knew it wasn't my idea.

Second, I'd been praying *exactly* for this—for a very practical, and different, remedy for each one of my concerns. Just because it was a remedy I would never have dared consider on my own didn't mean it wasn't valid. In fact, this made it all the more likely that the direction was from the Lord.

Third, as scary as this prospect was, I had very real peace about it. Forty hours a week would enable me to work and still be present with my family and friends, do ministry, invest in my relationship with the Lord, and enjoy some downtime—all the while limiting my destructive tendencies. Setting aside time for rest and relationships was completely biblical and would keep my focus in the right place. Additionally, without sales goals there would be no numeric results of my own making to strive for. I'd be letting God set the metrics.

The pervading peace and courage I had in the face of my fear was the deciding factor. Even though I'd be going against the grain—doing what my friends and business peers would never advise—I knew I didn't need their approval. Only the Lord's.

I reasoned that this had to be His answer. For four years He had been delivering on His promise to direct my steps. For four years He had been guiding me away from my own understanding and toward His. Now I had a choice: Would I move forward in faith? Stall out in fear? Or shift into reverse and do as I'd always done?

It was time to try something different and execute on Someone Else's plan.

CHAPTER 4

MY FIRST TEST RUN

I N RETROSPECT, THE CRAZINESS of this idea forced me to entrust any success to the Lord. It was like when God told ancient Israel's leader, Gideon: "You have too many men going into battle. If you defeat the enemy with such an army, the people will boast in their own strength." So He instructed Gideon regarding which men to send home, reducing the numbers from thirty-two thousand to three hundred warriors and saying, "Then you will know that your victory is because of me" (Judges 7:2, my paraphrase).

By all accounts, forty hours a week for a business startup was ridiculous. No entrepreneur in his or her right mind would consider it. But I had to put my trust in God because this seemed to be His answer to combat my enemy—my own flesh and old habits. I didn't know if the business would succeed, but I knew He could make it thrive in just forty hours a week if He chose to, and I could have a life outside the office on that same schedule. I needed to try His way and see what happened. (I'm not saying that everyone should work forty hours a week, though I do recommend asking the Lord where your boundary lines should fall. But at that point in time, I believe God wanted me to have faith first and foremost in Him, to counter my tendencies.)

When I did launch Texon in April of 1989, I was utterly aware that this faith experiment had no hope of working without Jesus as my Partner. That meant obeying the boundaries I believed He had set for me. I thought it was impossible to succeed if I didn't completely surrender to forty hours a week. I felt certain that if I disobeyed what I deemed was His specific solution for my situation, I would fail, either in my family relationships, or by burning out again, or worse.

If the failure of the business was God's will for me so that I could learn a greater lesson, then so be it, but I was determined not to let my dysfunction or my sin be the cause. And if things started to fail because I was getting in the way, I was willing to take steps to "pull the bad tooth" and address the problem before it got worse. The last thing I wanted was for my Partner to have to do something drastic to get my attention.

I felt so convicted in my desire to honor Jesus that, even to this day, I don't put in more than forty hours during the week—and I didn't back then either. As soon as I'd finished my eight hours on a given day, I was out the door.

I marvel now that I never tried to push that boundary, but this, too, was the Holy Spirit's doing. Yes, I had anxiety about whether I could make enough money for my family and me to live on with such a restricted schedule. In spite of that, though, God kept me at peace about obeying.

A Godly Pace

In this first real effort to slow my speed and wait for a peaceful answer from the Lord, I didn't know that what was being developed in me would be a multistep process that, more than three decades later, I would still be practicing. It was my initial test run at seeking to more clearly hear God and discern His will.

And now it's how I strive to get "in step" with God every time I make a big decision. By this I mean prayerfully and mindfully attempting to align my agenda, my schedule, and particularly my thoughts and desires, with His. I've so often fallen into the trap of hurrying my decisions and getting out ahead of His divine leadership. Other times, such as the years before my burnout, I've failed to consult Him at all. Working through these steps helps me not only seek God's direction but defer to His timing.

Until I was willing to downshift and wait for the Lord's answers, I didn't know I really could discover His plans for me, much less receive the desires of my heart. Yet for thirty years, it's been happening. And once I saw that this process had staying power, it became the way I discerned God's will for all the important decisions in my work and my life.

A Great Reward

The time it took to process through this situation showed me something else, something I was blind to for the first four decades of my life: God has a sacred pace all His own for the decisions of our lives, and every one of us needs His Holy Spirit to be able to discern it. In that sacred pace—in God's sovereign timing—His Spirit leads us to a sacred place: the center of God's will. Our part is to wait on the Lord with our eyes, ears, and hearts wide open.

I received an unbelievable reward six months into the launch of the company—a reward that had nothing to do with money. In fact, at that time, I was drawing no salary and we were yet to make a profit. To my surprise and delight, both of my daughters told me at dinner one night, "Dad, we don't know why you worried so much about this. You're the same as when you started Texon."

For Tanya and Jeannie to feel there had been no compromise in my priorities, no lessening of my time and attention toward them during the company's ramp-up, was so confirming—and so completely God! I cried later because only the Lord could give me such peace amid such a gamble.

That was the first of many blessings to come. And it was more than enough to keep me on this adventure with God.

Within eighteen months, Texon became profitable, and that has been true annually since then for twenty-nine consecutive years. I was so encouraged by this experience that when I came to another decision point, I again tried this approach of slowing down, listening for, and waiting on God—and yet again in other situations. Sure enough, whenever I put on the brakes and let the Holy Spirit navigate, I would ultimately be brought to a place of deep peace. For sure, there were detours and delays beyond my control (every road we travel has them), and my journey didn't always end up where I'd planned. Sometimes I arrived at a destination that wasn't anywhere on my map! Somehow, though, God used even the seeming setbacks to keep me moving in the right direction, and on His schedule, until His will and His way forward were clear to me.

For me to ever risk displeasing people by "moving outside the flow of traffic," so to speak—taking extra time to make decisions, sometimes going against the advice of my management team or against what might make sense economically—all because the Lord guided me otherwise? It has *not* come naturally for me. Nevertheless, that's how much things changed once I started listening for the Lord.

Upon realizing the difference this approach made in my business and the ripple effect it had in my relationships, I sought to reach a slower speed and get neutral in other areas of life as well. And now, no part of my life is exempt from its influence.

Not Natural, *Supernatural*

Starting any company is painful. Yet taking time to really bring all the factors to the Lord turned out so favorably that it dislodged me from my natural skepticism. I'm a bottom-line kind of guy who's made a living examining risk and reward. If the payoff isn't big enough, I scrap it. If it's a losing venture, I let it go. Had the payoff not been enormous, both short-term and long-term, I would have moved on to another approach a long time ago. Instead, I began routinely going into negotiations and business meetings with an ear toward discerning what God's pace and direction might be. Progressively, I identified four steps, each of which prepares me to more simply understand His decisions for me. And after all these years, my family, my health, my faith, and Texon as a company continue to see the sustained benefits of these deliberate attempts to slow myself down in order to align my will and schedule with the Lord's.

Clearly, for any of us to join pace with God and discern what He would have us do is not a natural process but a supernatural one. It's not the proverbial handwriting on the wall that we would all prefer, but it *is* from Him just the same, much like a map app tells you the best route depending on traffic.

Given how I very painfully arrived at this way of doing life and business, I'm still surprised that this is my go-to process for decision-making. I've relied on what I've gleaned from a daily study of God's Word, from my friendship with Jesus, and from integrating the spiritual practices of classic Christian writers like George Müller and Oswald Chambers.

Müller in particular was well known for prayerfully relying on God's day-to-day guidance as he and his wife fed, clothed, housed, and educated thousands of orphans in nineteenth-century England. He prayed about everything, took steps of faith when prompted by the Holy Spirit, and believed the Lord would answer in due time in all things. And God's timely responses to him are the stuff of legend, only they're true! He and his wife were able to accomplish their ongoing mission for decades without ever going into debt or soliciting donations. I'm pretty sure Müller would've said, "I couldn't manu-facture this on my own." In fact, he did say as much when he wrote: "Faith does not operate in the realm of the possible. There is no glory for God in that which is humanly possible. *Faith begins where man's power ends.*"[1]

CHAPTER 5
....

IN STEP WITH GOD

A FEW YEARS AGO, *Sports Illustrated* ran a "Holiday Help List" supplement that featured various gifts that would be of interest for athletic types. The description for a golf watch read:

> Equipped with a hi-res color touch screen, a GPS receiver, and 38,000 preloaded courses, it provides distances to and from any possible target or hazard. So you know what to aim for and what to avoid.[1]

If only downloading the Lord's will were that easy, right? Who doesn't want to know in advance which course to choose, what hazards lie ahead, and how close they are? In fact, I have a theory that we Christians want to obtain the Lord's direction for our decisions—if He would only make His guidance clear. Were we able to tap a watch and run the analytics to determine where the possibilities would take us, we'd be golden! But life is not so measurable. And God's thoughts and ways are a mystery to our finite minds.

So how do we as humans begin to fathom His plans? By slowing ourselves to His pace until we've gotten neutral. From there you can find your bearings and discern how and when to proceed through any crossroads in the Lord's instructions.

We will work through each part of my process in the next section, but as an introduction, the steps are:

1. Consult your Friend Jesus.
2. Gather the facts.
3. Watch for circumstances.
4. Get neutral.

While I've numbered the steps and will speak of them in this order for ease of reference, getting on God's pace is rarely a linear progression. In fact, the first three steps are often more like three streams running together until they converge into the "river" of Step 4. At that getting neutral point—after you've prayerfully spent time in God's presence, obtained His perspective based on all the information at hand, and broken free from your own agenda—you're ready for His answer. Whenever He delivers His answer, signaled by a sure peace deep inside, you do it. *This* is when you start to move forward again.

Because the Lord is guiding the entire process, it's important to let Him determine the order of the steps. The Holy Spirit may guide you to repeat one step multiple times before moving you to another, or direct you across multiple steps at the same time. He certainly did both with me in the decision to start Texon. What's important to remember is that God's leading is not separate from any single step of the process; He can and will use any and all the steps to indicate His plans for you.

Easy Does It

Think of this entire process as easing off the rush of your desires until you are objective. Not so driven by ungodly influences or worldly demands. Wide open to the Lord's best for you. If you understand it in this positive sense, then you can see how the decision to slow your pace allows the first three steps to lead you to the fourth and final step of getting neutral, where you are perfectly positioned to receive the gift of God's will and, ultimately, to act on it.

All four steps were very real elements of my decision to start Texon, though admittedly so organic that I didn't know they were leading to a lifelong process for decision-making. With my penchant for acceleration, it's probably good that I didn't know I would need three full years before being ready to receive God's decision that very first time. Nonetheless, I found the four steps to be extremely positive—energizing, not disheartening.

The entire process of seeking God's pace was immersed in prayer (Step 1) from beginning to end. That's initially all I knew to do— hit the brakes and beg God for His mercy and wisdom. In time, though, as I developed a friendship with Jesus (Step 1), more of a give-and-take occurred. As I brought Him into this decision, it felt as if He brought me into the work that was underway in my life. I never stopped asking Him to change and heal me, but at the same time my eyes were opened to things I could do, such as implementing new routines and habits to help safeguard myself and my family. I suppose that shouldn't have surprised me: since the days in Eden, God has given His people work to do in partnership with Him. But it did surprise me. It excited me, too, because as I was learning to trust Him, He seemed to be entrusting me with more responsibility. I certainly longed to be a good steward of this fresh start!

Joining in the process with Him produced an additional aware-ness and consideration of both the facts and the circumstances surrounding this decision. Essentially, I transferred the careful due diligence of my business deals to my spiritual life. At this slower spiri-tual pace, I had time to gather and weigh the facts of my situation (Step 2). As you've read, I wasn't only evaluating the economics of starting my own business; I also considered the emotional toll on my family and the physical and spiritual costs to my health if I continued doing business as I'd always done it. I also sought the counsel of other Christians, giving them permission to speak truth to me and make sure I didn't misinterpret the "data" of my life.

Becoming more aware of unfolding circumstances (Step 3)— the events and decisions that were outside of my control—gave me a better eye for God's hand in them, knowing they either derive from Him or are allowed by Him. And soon my own responses started to change. Rather than perceiving setbacks (such as Ken's departure from my life) as delays to my destination, I could recognize them as God's handiwork: Him closing doors *for me*, moving me that much closer to the one He already had standing wide open. Instead of trying to sell Bill on letting me develop new business, or going behind his back and asking forgiveness later, I could more readily accept his no and listen for the new possibilities God might want to impart to me.

God used these first three steps to help open my heart to that vital question: "What do You want me to do, Jesus?" This was crucial for, in time, something very unexpected happened: I found that my will was graciously neutralized, and I actually wanted what *He* wanted more than any solution of mine (Step 4). This also enabled me to wait and continue praying for the Lord's will to be done until the Holy Spirit quietly guided me to a better way than anything I'd come up with: forty-hour workweeks and no sales goals. And though it was not at all the answer I'd anticipated, I had a peace that couldn't be shaken, in spite of the risks involved, which strengthened my resolve to act on it exactly as I'd been led.

In my decisions even now, these various efforts to listen to God either confirm the pointers He has indicated or help me realize that I'm headed in the wrong direction and need to recalculate. Thus, my best GPS is my God Positioning System. "It is God making [us] wise," says pastor Tim Keller. "If God seems to be leading my heart to a no when lots of other indicators are saying yes, then I figure He'll show me that the other indicators are wrong."[2]

Practice, Practice

Getting in step with God will take some practice, some getting used to. So will learning to recognize the Spirit's voice versus our own. As Chris Tiegreen rightly admits:

> We have difficulty distinguishing between our God-given but distorted consciences and the pure, convicting voice of our Lord. The Spirit of God dwells within us, but so do all sorts of misconceptions, anxieties, phobias, hang-ups, and habits. When we think we hear His voice, is it a matter of revelation or psychosis? In our discernment, there is a fine line between the two. In the reality of His kingdom, there is an unbridgeable division between them. We must learn how to tell the difference. That is why a strict adherence to God's Word is paramount.[3]

God's Word is paramount because, as our unchanging source of wisdom and truth, it contains all the coordinates we will ever need for getting from point A to point B in each situation of our lives. It's the platform for our entire navigational system; without it, we will never see the places we hope to see in our life's journey.

Tiegreen continues:

> As our minds go through . . . the transformation from old, worldly ways of thinking to grasping and embodying the deep mysteries of the now-revealed Kingdom of God—we must saturate them in His words. His teaching must become the first set of criteria used in our decision-making. His wisdom must become the fire that melts us and the mold that shapes us.[4]

God's Word shows us what to do, gives us the power to do it, and increases our faith *as* we do it. Through daily Bible reading and time spent in prayer and other spiritual disciplines (such as devotional reading and meditating on and memorizing Scripture), our day-to-day spiritual life is nurtured—and before we know it, a robust faith has surfaced.

To stay on God's pace means staying connected to the Vine, who is Christ. Jesus extended this invitation to every follower: "Remain in me, and I will remain in you. . . . I am the vine; you are the branches. Those who remain in me, and I in them, will produce much fruit" (John 15:4–5, NLT). As I genuinely seek Him, I find myself abiding in, remaining in, and relying on Him more and more. And that connectedness bears spiritual fruit in my life and decisions.

When I don't regularly take time with Him, I weaken and lose my way. I lose sight of what He intends for me and what He thinks of me. I start focusing on the world and listening to its messages instead. I have to take time with Jesus, away from the frantic pace and demands of my life. That's what His sacred pace is for. It gives every believer an opportunity to commune with Him as Friend and really hear the whispers of the Holy Spirit. He is that necessary guiding voice—a living voice, not a preprogrammed one like we find on our smartphones—offering turn-by-turn instructions to keep God's people on the best route for both the conditions we're in and the conditions to come. In other words, personalized, proactive help is available to every man or woman of God who is willing to listen.

Slowing down is key. When faced with a decision, instead of going faster, as we're inclined to do, the goal is to learn to adopt a slower pace until you have completed the fourth and final step, that unique and critical step of getting neutral, where you desire God's will over your own. From this openhearted, openhanded position, God's answer can be most clearly heard and most boldly obeyed. It is both where we hear Him best and where we can receive His best.

Keeping It Simple

Not only do these steps flow together (with some practice) to reveal God's will, but not one of them is complicated. In fact, among my favorite things about this process is that it's simple. That doesn't mean "always easy" or "painless," but it does mean less complicated—and able to be applied no matter where you are in your faith journey. It actually simplifies situations that our human emotions or impulses tend to make very complex, and it helps clarify where we may be pursuing the wrong answer or the wrong agenda in the first place.

I read somewhere that "God loves to communicate Himself to simple people," and I feel I'm about as uncomplicated as a person can be. So if the Lord can get through to me in such a life-changing way, I trust that He will speak to you on your own terms as you read.

I won't mislead you, however. *What's in this book is not for the faint of heart.* The process outlined in these pages is easy to understand but will require real effort (and possibly some significant changes) on your part.

You'll need emotional courage—a willingness to be fiercely real with yourself, call your sin what it is, and relentlessly fight your dragons. It's quite a painful thing to dig deep into your motives and find that damaged roots exist. It's no fun to admit your anger, your pride, your selfishness or greed, and then to have to wrestle those emotions into submission before you make a move. But this is critical for gaining "the ears to hear" that Jesus so often spoke of.

You'll also need a measure of faith—both in God's Word and through the nudges of the Holy Spirit. This means acting in faith once you have peace that the answer is from the Lord, even if that next step scares you or is vastly different from what you expected. It also means waiting patiently for Him, regardless of how other people might be pressuring you to speed up. I like the way one writer explains it: "Patience doesn't mean making a pact with the devil of denial, ignoring our emotions and aspirations. It means being wholeheartedly engaged in the process that's unfolding, rather than . . . ripping open a budding flower [or] demanding a caterpillar hurry up and get that chrysalis stage over with."[5]

Delivered!

What God's sacred pace delivers us from is not just our "need for speed" but the trouble that comes from relying on our own shortsighted understanding. I often remind myself: "Don't trust yourself—the devil loves for you to play God." I am playing God when I choose not to seek His help or admit my limitations.

We receive Christ's perfect strength when we are weak (2 Cor. 12:9). What a wonderful promise from Him when we are struggling! The reality we may be reluctant to admit, however, is that we cannot succeed without His help. Seventeenth-century theologian John Owen recognized, "We can have no power from Christ, unless we live in a persuasion that we have none of our own."[6] Jesus said in John 15:5: "Apart from me you can do nothing." He wasn't using hyperbole; He meant *nothing*.

It's not so hard to agree with Christ when we're in the weeds, without a clue about what we're doing. It's harder to confess in areas where we are proficient, humanly speaking. If I'm already pretty good at something, I get in this mindset that I don't need the Lord. I may not even think about Him when troubles arise, simply because *I'm a pro at this; I can figure it out*. Consequently, I'm prone to keep pressing ahead in my own knowledge rather than slowing down to seek His.

Relying on God means consulting Him and letting Him lead, period. The more competent I am in an area of decision, the less likely I am to draw on the Lord because, in my own flesh, I think I'm sufficient. I forget to go to Him in my areas of giftedness. Moving at God's pace, however, means consulting—and waiting on—the real Expert of everything to weigh in.

Try this little exercise for some perspective the next time you're faced with a decision. Draw a circle and place a dot in the center, then honestly ask yourself: "If this circle represents my world, who does the dot represent?" For most of us, there are only two honest answers: *God* or *Me*. I put this question to a young unbeliever very recently, and he did not want to say "Me" because he was so generous toward others. And yet in all honesty, he knew he couldn't say "God" either. We Christians probably interchange the answer depending on the situation or our stress level, but slowing down to a lesser speed increases the chances that we will remember who knows best and re-center our hearts and plans where they belong.

Being aware of our need for God is our greatest strength. When we lean on Him, we can do anything that He has planned and purposed for us to do. Exchanging our weakness for the Lord's strength enables us to avoid making the mistake that the psalmist decried: "Unless the Lord builds the house, the builders labor in vain" (Ps. 127:1). Think of it: A life in vain. A business in vain. Relationships in vain. This is what our little kingdoms come to if we strive to accomplish anything minus our true Strength.

CHAPTER 6
....

TRUST AND BELIEVE

A CONSULTANT WE ONCE hired said that successful people and businesses rarely know what makes them successful; they just do what they do.

Those words were true of Texon corporately for a very long time, although we've since worked hard to be able to articulate what we do best and why. Those words were also descriptive of me with this decision-making process until just recently. For years, I never wrote out my steps; I just operated in them when making decisions. I actually didn't even share the process with anyone until about 2008. That's when I finally got up the guts to ask a ministry leader, "Will you give me five minutes and let me tell you how the Lord leads me in my decisions? Is this crazy?"

His response was, "It sounds biblical to me."

That freed me to start speaking of this process to other people. The idea of slowing my speed until I get neutral didn't originate with me (though my therapist does remember when I came up with the phrase *getting neutral*); the process itself actually flows from established prayer traditions introduced to me by him. Yet while the concept isn't mine, its application in my life is. After my burnout, it was almost as if the Holy Spirit sorted through these heady prayer traditions and helped me apply them in very down-to-earth steps, not only for my own sake, but also, I believe, with the expectation that I would teach them to others.

I want everyone to be able to discern and do the will of God, experiencing the blessings of obeying Him. Having the faith to downshift and follow a process until you're neutral can lead to a practical, simple walk with Jesus and a joyous life centered in God's will. This is at the heart of why I wanted to write this book: Jesus said a mature, surrendered Christian can move mountains with the faith he or she has—and I've found this process to be a great faith builder.

Laying the Foundation

For me, Proverbs 3:5–6 is my entire four-step process in a nutshell: "Trust in the LORD with all your heart, and lean not on your own understanding; in all your ways acknowledge Him, and He shall direct your paths" (NKJV). *The Message* version of the Bible says it even more simply: "Trust GOD from the bottom of your heart; don't try to figure out everything on your own. Listen for GOD's voice in everything you do, everywhere you go; he's the one who will keep you on track."

This passage lays the foundation not only for slowing down to a sacred pace, but also for actually getting neutral:

- Trust in the Lord, not yourself.
- Trust in His sovereign knowledge, not your limited understanding of present circumstances or your assumptions about the future.
- Trust in the Lord with all your heart. Bill Blocker, president of the College of Biblical Studies in Houston, says that "heart" here "refers to both an intellectual and volitional trust that is not swayed by emotions or impulsive reactions to circumstances."[1] This is the place of wholeness where the Spirit of the Lord speaks unfiltered answers.

- Look to (acknowledge) Him in *all* your ways—meaning, not just when you clearly need help, and not just in the areas that are out of your hands anyway, but in everything you are considering. The Lord sees the future. In full. Right down to the last detail. Let Him show you which way to go.
- Believe and expect that He will be true to His promise to not only direct your steps personally but to clear the road ahead so you can live in the security of His plans.

Believing God's Promises

I suspect a major reason I was able to believe this promise of God in Proverbs 3 is because, several years prior, I'd taken up His challenge on another biblical promise, and He had proven utterly faithful to His Word.

Malachi 3:10 was that testing ground for me. It was tangible, and its guarantee is straight from the Lord. God told His people: "Bring the whole tithe into the storehouse, that there may be food in my house. *Test me in this* . . . and see if I will not throw open the floodgates of heaven and pour out so much blessing that there will not be room enough to store it" (emphasis mine).

I read this passage before becoming a Christian (in fact, about six months before my burnout). Knowing a great deal when I saw one, I was immediately on board. *I give away 10 percent of what I make, and I get all these blessings from the windows of heaven? I'll take that offer!* It was purely self-serving at the time. Yet I knew I could do that simple thing of tithing a portion of my income—and I sure wanted the reward!

After I became a Christian, I heard Dr. Stanley Tam speak at a prayer breakfast for businesspeople in Houston. The founder of U.S. Plastic Corporation, he had written a book titled *God Owns My Business*, and he shared that he gave 50 percent of his income to charities and ministries. Texon was not in my vision at the time, but I thought, *If Jesus Christ can give His life for me, I can give my earnings back to Him.* So I made Dr. Tam's example one of my goals. And progressively, over thirteen years, Doris and I increased our giving from an initial 10 percent of my annual income to 20 percent, then 30 percent. Finally, by mid-1998, we were giving away 50 percent of my gross income.

Believing the promise of Malachi 3:10 brought me to such a great place! Giving generously and cheerfully pleased God and gave me joy. And as I delighted in the Lord in this way, He enabled me to fulfill one of the primary desires of my heart: helping ministries around the world to fulfill their missions.

When we trust God in one thing, He multiplies the fruit of our obedience and strengthens the roots of our faith. Consequently, that first time I actually got neutral, establishing Texon on only a forty-hour workweek with no sales goals, I could dare to believe His answer because He had proved faithful in my initial decision to tithe.

I have come to hold in my soul that what the Bible says is true: When we ask our Father in heaven for bread, He won't hand us a stone. When we ask with the right motives, He gives; when we seek Him, He makes sure we find (Matt. 7:7–11). There are so many biblical truths like these that belong in our personal archives. But it wasn't enough to be satisfied with only storing them up; I had to be ready to stand on those unfailing words.

We don't do this alone, in our own strength. We can't. The Holy Spirit is the One who empowers us to both understand the words of God and to take Him at His word.

Jesus said, "Everyone who hears these words of mine *and puts them into practice* is like a wise man who built his house on the rock" (Matt. 7:24, emphasis mine). One writer has elaborated:

> We are to hear [Jesus'] voice clearly. And Jesus offers it clearly. He has instructed us thoroughly. He has shed His light on the Old

Testament—it is all summed up in Him—and He has shined His light into the New. . . . We must define truth by Him and define all that is outside of Him as untruth. We must build all our houses on the solid, unshakable foundation of His Kingdom.[2]

I had often read the Bible over the years without putting any weight on its truths. Yet how else will you test what God has said? Somewhere along the way, you have to see if His words hold. So I started with what I *did* believe, as small as it may have been, and essentially asked God to grow that sapling into an oak tree. I began with these questions:

First, do I believe God in general? Believe that He doesn't lie and that He has good plans for me? We all know people who have let us down. Is it possible, though, that the One who knit me in detail in my mother's womb could be reliable? I decided: *Why not give Him a chance?*

Second, do I believe that His Word, the Bible, is fundamentally true, giving an accurate account of our world, our hearts, ancient history, and the life and teachings of Christ? I wasn't clear on all the details, and I still had questions about certain things. Overall, however, was I convinced that the Bible tells it like it is?

Because I could affirm these two things, the words and truths and principles of God were already in transit from my head to my heart—which is the farthest distance in the world. As long as they stayed only words on a page, just verses clanging around in my head, they had little to no impact on my life or my decisions. Once I absorbed them, they strengthened me like nutrients to my soul.

Change comes and faith rises when you live out the truths of God. You simply have to try. If you're uncertain about the Lord's reliability, then let my experiences with Him be an example. Better yet, read the experiences of all those men and women who are mentioned in the biblical Hall of Faith in Hebrews 11. Either way, test Him out! Prove any of us wrong! God is willing to guide your steps to receive His gifts. Trust Him enough to let Him.

A New Understanding

John Patchell is CEO of a natural-gas service company in Houston, and he has found Romans 12:2 to be his biblical call to God's divine pace: "Do not be conformed to this world, but be transformed by the renewing of your mind, that you may prove [for yourselves] what is that good and acceptable and perfect will of God" (NKJV). Biblical commentators say that to "prove" God's will means to work to discern the right course of action from His perspective and then to do it. This discerning and doing "is the end result," explains John. "It's what I'm going for. I'm always wanting the will without doing the work. But the work comes first."[3]

The work involves training ourselves to think differently. We have to sacrifice our self-reliance. We have to reset our understanding to this: we are not all-knowing, we are not all-loving, and we are not all-seeing. Only God is. Until we are willing to live according to this reality, we will not begin to shift to His sacred timing, much less get neutral about anything.

One of the cofounders of Desiring God Ministries explains the human condition in this way:

> So many of the things that cause us the most difficulty and heartache in life, the source of so much of our anxiety, fear, doubt, and anger with others and with God, is the result of leaning on our own understanding. . . .
>
> In . . . trusting fully in the Lord and not leaning on our own understanding—we're not setting aside our intellect. We're resting our intellect upon the intellect of God. Nothing is wiser or saner. To do so is to allow him to direct our paths, which not only lead to ultimate joy, but also make the journey itself, even when laden with sorrow, joyful (2 Corinthians 6:10). And it preserves for us all the

pleasures God provides us in the world. To not do this is the height of foolishness and the path to misery.[4]

Another writer states:

> If we ever take hold of the idea that we are innately wise, we are destined for failure. . . . Placing any faith in our own wisdom is a form of pride. It is also self-delusion. We do not know anything about the future for certain; we don't know the intricacies of our own hearts; we don't see all the motives and moods of other people . . . and we don't fully grasp the spiritual realities of God's Kingdom. . . . To act as if the reverse is true is the ultimate foolishness.[5]

Most importantly, Scripture repeatedly affirms the unmatched wisdom of God: "The fear of the LORD is the beginning of wisdom, and knowledge of the Holy One is understanding" (Prov. 9:10; see also Ps. 111:10 and Prov. 1:7). The kind of fear mentioned in that verse is that of reverence or respect—what happens when you acknowledge someone as a reliable authority. Understanding God as that reliable authority (a wise Father), then how old am I by comparison?

If I'm honest, I'm no older than age two or three in my knowledge of the answers for my life. God's experience, wisdom, and perspective are so vast that it's laughable for me to try to make decisions without Him. And yet, you know how, when you're a kid, you believe that the world centers around you and that you know best? Well, even we adults can take on that attitude if we're not careful. We often behave like children with our heavenly Father—striving to have our way, convinced we should have everything we please, prone to temper tantrums and foolish choices—all because we trust ourselves and not the Lord.

The difference is, as adults our choices sometimes come with awful consequences that may affect not only us but the people we care about most. A two-year-old in real life is not going to cost people their jobs or cause a divorce or ruin sensitive negotiations. But an adult with a two-year-old's mentality and foolish self-reliance is capable of any of these things.

King Solomon, who is historically understood as the wisest man who ever lived, wrote, "The way of fools seems right to them, but the wise listen to advice" (Prov. 12:15). Not surprisingly, his wisdom came from the Lord. God made an incredible, Aladdin-like offer to Solomon as he was becoming the next king in ancient Israel: "Ask for whatever you want me to give you." And the young king's answer was almost as remarkable: "I am only a little child and do not know how to carry out my duties. . . . So give your servant a discerning heart to govern your people and to distinguish between right and wrong. For who is able to govern this great people of yours?" (1 Kings 3:5, 7, 9).

Because Solomon asked for wisdom rather than power or possessions, the Lord granted his desire—and then so much more—giving him wealth and fame like no one, not even Bill Gates, has ever seen.

Becoming Wise

If my burnout taught me anything, it's that eating the fruit of your own wisdom is always a bitter experience. So how do you obtain God's wisdom in order to avoid the kinds of regrets that can haunt you? As James 1:5 says, just ask: "If any of you lacks wisdom, you should ask God, who gives generously to all without finding fault, and it will be given to you."

One writer has called this particular request "a prayer . . . that should come before all our other prayers." He goes on to say:

> We can ask God to put His thoughts into our minds and His will into our hearts. We are not asking for Him simply to point the way; we are asking for Him to infuse His way into the very depths

of our souls. We are asking for His Spirit to direct us from within. We are praying to receive His mind as our own.

Most assuredly, this is an answerable prayer. God waits with anticipation for us to ask it. He encourages it and appeals for it, calling us into it repeatedly. He doesn't just want to pass on His information to us; He wants to fill us with Himself. Then our desires become His, His plans are written into our dreams, and He lives the life of His Spirit in the body of our flesh. It's a powerful communion, amazing in its mercy.[6]

As you've read, it took about three years before I was in a place—emotionally and spiritually—where I could be open to God's solution for how to start a company and still honor my family. But my burnout made me more willing to rely on a wisdom outside of myself.

Pastor John Ortberg has written: "A coachable spirit is core to wisdom."[7] How do I know when I'm ready to listen? When my inner toddler wants to sit at the feet of the wizened, doting Father that I understand God to be, and soak in whatever He has to say, sure that He can be trusted.

Admittedly, God's answers and methods don't always make sense. They don't always fit the world's wisdom and rationale. They aren't pleasurable each and every moment. But He has designed them as mile markers to your next destination, and these mile markers lead to glorious places if you will follow them all the way to the end. You may encounter some speed bumps and some crazy, hairpin curves in the road, but you have the assurance that every one of them is there for a purpose: to bring you to dream locations and lead you to the most magnificent views.

For those who will dare to depend on God's wisdom rather than their own, He promises to clear their path of any obstacles that would ultimately rob them of their joy. This includes the ones we construct ourselves. In the heart that is surrendered to Him, God faithfully works to clear out both closets and corners—any place that a person might be hiding dysfunction or sin that could keep them from His beautiful best. Once the Spirit of God has done His work, we can trust that the only obstacles remaining are sovereignly appointed ones: what we will individually need to receive and savor the Lord's will.

Divine Peace

The Bible says that God signals His answers by a confirming peace within. This peace is your green light to move forward, with the Lord's blessing.

God's peace is very much an *in spite of* peace—a calm, undeniable knowing and empowering in spite of your circumstances, limitations, or fears. The Amplified Bible speaks of it as "[that peace which reassures the heart, that peace] which transcends all understanding, [that peace which] stands guard over your hearts and your minds in Christ Jesus" (Phil. 4:7).

It's difficult to explain because of its supernatural origin; in any case, when you have it, you *have* it! God confirms His way with a settledness, an assurance, that can't be humanly produced. And He supplies the courage you need to act on His instructions. You may still feel some trepidation, but He provides enough peace and confidence for you to move forward with His plan.

Who to Trust

No human being can comprehend the vastness of God's knowledge or His love. He knows the start to the finish in everything—including our entire life story and the details of our current dilemma. He cares most about our best, and His answer is the only one we need. So it only makes sense that we should pause to hear His advice before speeding ahead into the next adventure.

Life comes down to a matter of who we trust. On the one hand, it's a no-brainer if we're talking about ability. The Bible tells us God is able to do beyond whatever we can ask or even imagine (Eph. 3:20). Yet our real issue is usually not whether He *can* be good to us; we mostly struggle with whether He *will*. We tend to view God as being fickle, don't we? As if He only fulfills His promises when He feels like it—or if we've performed to His expectations. Oh, how we need to understand how faithful and loving He is!

In our humanness, deciding who to trust doesn't come easily. So here's a little logic for this all-important decision: whatever your inner two-year-old might have to give up at the moment to trust the wisdom of God is nothing compared to the hurt you're headed for if you persist in ignoring His wisdom. The consequences of relying on yourself are severe. Why not take the less painful option? Confer with the Lord. I promise you, He sovereignly knows and delivers what's best—and what will bring you joy. Even better, He *wants* you to have His very best because He loves you so much.

Here's one more thing that might help you: practice trusting Him. Trust is a muscle that we must exercise. Training yourself to rely on His wisdom rather than yours is no joke. I know of a very accomplished man who has gone several months without a job, in spite of sending out dozens of résumés and having numerous interviews. One of these days, when he does receive a job offer, can you imagine the competition between his own wisdom and the Lord's if, upon finally getting neutral, the Holy Spirit whispers, "Don't take that job"?

Times like those are when you have to put feet to your faith—*going* without *knowing* every part of the plan.[8] You will probably never completely silence the noise in your head that tells you to do what makes sense to you. But you can train yourself to decelerate and listen to the Wise One who has a timeless track record of being right. If you're like me, your impulses have a sketchy history. But God's performance record? Flawless. You just aren't capable of knowing or doing what's best if you're not listening to Him.

The psalmist knew the way to wisdom: "I will listen to what God the LORD says; he promises peace to his people, his faithful servants—but let them not turn to folly" (Ps. 85:8). Have you come to grips with the limits of your understanding? The beginning of wisdom is exactly this: trust God, who knows all, rather than yourself or your own know-how. From this starting point, His sacred pace comes more naturally.

His Speed for Our Good

God has His own speed for our good and for His purposes! What might it look like for you to be operating at His pace? What might it take for you to be willing to wait on God's timing to gain His will for your life? Can you trust Him? Do you believe He is actually at work while you are waiting?

Proverbs 16:2 says, "All a person's ways seem pure to them, but motives are weighed by the LORD." With the four steps we'll be examining in the next section, I'm able to:

- strip away the layers to discern what's really going on inside me,
- confess and work through anything that is hindering me from whatever God wants of me, and
- filter down to the heart of the matter—what's most important—and act on *that* rather than my fears or selfish whims.

And you know what? When I take the time to do this, so that I'm trusting God with my whole heart, decisions become clearer. Unique solutions are revealed that I hadn't thought of before. Circumstances work out for the good, even when they don't initially go my way. And best of all, He gives me peace about what to do. Just as He promised.

He will do the same for you.

Sacred Pace at a Glance

Three Key Verses

Delight yourself in the LORD, and he will
give you the desires of your heart.
—Ps. 37:4, ESV

Trust in the LORD with all your heart, and lean
not on your own understanding; in all your ways
acknowledge Him, and He shall direct your paths.
—Prov. 3:5–6, NKJV

Do not conform to the pattern of this world, but be
transformed by the renewing of your mind. Then
you will be able to test and approve what God's
will is—his good, pleasing and perfect will.
—Rom. 12:2

Three Core Truths

- God knows best, and I only think I do.
- He sees the future, and I can't.
- He loves me and everyone around
  me more than I ever could.

Four Steps

- *Step 1:* Consult your Friend Jesus.
- *Step 2:* Gather the facts.
- *Step 3:* Watch for circumstances.
- *Step 4:* Get neutral.

PART 2

FOUR STEPS TO A
SACRED PACE

CHAPTER 7

STEP 1: CONSULT YOUR FRIEND JESUS

I F MY LIFE PROVES anything, it's that we often approach the Lord with our minds already made up. In those instances, we're actually not engaging Jesus at all; we're asking Him to sign off on our wishes. I'm not saying we do this consciously, but it's very easy to fall into this trap. Especially if we have not learned to vigorously question ourselves.

To consult Jesus in prayer as the first step in our decisions helps to "unmake" our minds.

It allows time for the Great Revealer, the Holy Spirit, to peel away the layers and expose not only our true desires but all the ways we've covered them over. It softens our hearts and inclines our ears toward Jesus. Reminds us that we are not God. And opens our eyes to our real intentions.

Why Jesus?

You may wonder why I've specified Jesus here. While theologians generally agree that we can seek out any member of the Trinity for help—God the Father, Christ the Son, or the Holy Spirit—I focus this chapter on Jesus for a few reasons.

First of all, I want everyone who reads this book to know how good and loving He is. Second, having been "God with us" up close and personal, He can relate to us and us to Him. He walked among us on this earth; wore a physical body with its temptations and hungers, needs, and wants; and faced exactly the kinds of struggles that we do—yet without any failing. This makes Him a wonderful role model and example. Finally, I focus this chapter on Jesus because what really elevated my faith to the next level as a new Christian was making a new friend. And not just any friend, but the One who would become my Friend and Business Partner, Jesus. His unlimited love and acceptance toward me altered my life in every way.

After I tried for so long to fill the hole inside of me with money, success, and people pleasing, God gave me the faith (through much pain) to start looking to Jesus, and nothing has been the same. As I grew still, opening myself day after day to His love and direction, I began to see Jesus as never before. The more I talked with Him in prayer, the more my heart and mind changed. And as they did, I was able to turn from my old ways of thinking and be in a position for His will—and especially His own heart toward me—to be clearly revealed.

Experiencing Christ's Love

Therapy got the ball rolling, helping me to understand that my entire identity had been wrapped up in a desperate quest to succeed and please others. During these intensive sessions, the insecurities and sinful pride behind all my striving were laid bare. Meanwhile, God's Word was transforming my mind, helping me discover the Terry Looper whom God had created rather than the straw man my upbringing and my own rush of desires had constructed.

Freshly aware that I'd never felt truly, unconditionally loved by anyone, I longed even more for the Lord to let me experience His love for me. The little boy in me deeply desired it, and the man I was needed it, because I didn't want to exist on head knowledge anymore. I craved an expression of love that would penetrate my heart and settle deeply into my soul, and so I humbly asked God for just that.

My prayer was answered many months after my burnout, while Doris and I were vacationing at a hotel on the beach in San Diego. Nothing dramatic preceded the moment. I was simply lying in bed one morning, praying and enjoying the quiet as the ocean waves played their rhythm outside our window. In that peaceful setting, I felt myself being embraced by an overwhelming warmth and tenderness that, even years later, I have trouble putting into words. There was so much affection and acceptance in it, I couldn't stop crying. I knew that Jesus was with me and that He noticed me. *Really* noticed me. It was what the little boy in me had always wanted from my parents; now I was receiving it from the One who sacrificed His life for me.

Doris saw a real difference in me after that. She says this is when I finally understood I didn't need to be perfect to be accepted by God. This experience of unexpected love was so personal and so profound that it opened the door for me to understand Jesus not only as my Lord and Savior but as a real Friend with whom I could discuss any concern or challenge.

Relating to Him as I would any close friend—where there is trust, devotion, honesty, and frequent communication—had a great impact beyond my prayer life. For one, it later made getting neutral in my decisions a whole lot easier. Relating to Him so personally also helped me start applying God's Word more personally, as written to me directly, not just to humanity at large.

Letting Jesus love me altered my love for others too. Now that absolutely everything was new in my eyes, I was eager for everything to be made new in my world. His great love made me even more zealous to restore the damage I'd done to my relationships. Yet it was obvious that I had a lot of work to do to regain people's trust, particularly within my own family.

For example, it took about three years of me being present in my youngest daughter's life before she stopped being wary of my motives. My therapist would tell me, "Just hang out with your girls." I didn't know how at first, but Doris encouraged me: "Go sit on the floor in Jeannie's room while she's in there. She'll talk to you."

Eventually she did start talking, and as we connected, those occasional conversations turned into frequent ones. By the time Jeannie graduated from high school, she and I had eaten breakfast together nearly every day since her eighth-grade year. It didn't make up for all the dinners I'd missed when she was younger, but I'm grateful she was willing to forge this tradition with me. Picking up my eldest, Tanya, after her gymnastics practices and going by the donut shop afterward also allowed us to establish a new relationship. These are some of my best memories ever.

Christ rebuilt my relationship with my wife as well. Doris and I were so into our "new" marriage (a marriage that was then nearing twenty years) that we would go away for a weekend every other month or so to take inventory and talk. We never knew what the time would be like—whether it would be quiet and prayerful, physically intimate, or tinged with disagreement—but when we left, we would often remark to each other how worthwhile it was.

I've heard of others becoming more whole in their soul just by experiencing Jesus' love too. Sadly, based on the number of Christians I've spoken to about this, it's apparently not unusual to go many years (or an entire lifetime!) without a deep sense of our Lord's love. Rather than excitedly crawling up on Jesus' lap as we can imagine the children in the Gospels doing, we remain guarded, distant. We're wary of being hurt. Scared that we may not be lovable. As a result, a lot of people do what I did: they get busy "being Christian"—doing and performing to gain Christ's approval—if they don't give up on Him altogether.

Prayer brings us close and starts to reestablish trust. It is conversation; it is attention and affection passing between heaven and earth. It is what enables us to let Jesus' wholehearted love in. His delight is felt most freely when we approach Him with open arms.

To engage with Jesus as a real person rather than a vague concept took away so much pressure for me. It wasn't about me being good enough anymore. I no longer flippantly viewed Him as my spiritual Santa Claus either. Yes, He cared to do kind things for me; yes, He was generous to me; but now it was about slowing down to enjoy the sweetness of friendship and connect deeply with Him. I was realizing that Jesus really wants to be my Friend—He is invested in helping me figure out this thing called life, and He never, ever turns me away.

When I understood this in my soul, I understood it is no more self-serving to befriend Him than it is to share your life with anyone you love. Jesus wants intimacy and relationship! He is excited and pleased when we invite Him into our lives.

Relationship, Not Concept

Maybe you've been missing out on the relationship He wants with you. Maybe you're afraid of Him, convinced He wants nothing to do with you because of something in your past. Or maybe you've spent way too long in that empty space where you're relating to some vague idea of God rather than the person of Jesus Christ. But you will never feel the love of a concept.

Love is a relational word. To experience unconditional acceptance, straight from the heart of the One who loves you most, is the seed from which all good things grow. Once I knew Jesus, once His love penetrated my heart, the fruit of His Spirit blossomed. I had more love, more joy, more peace, more patience—and I was never the same.

A staffer at a Christian camp one summer confessed to me, "My marriage isn't good."

I asked, "Have you ever felt Jesus' love?"

"I've sure seen it," he said.

"But have you ever felt and known it for yourself?" I pressed.

"Well, no."

"When you do, your marriage will be changed," I told him. "I don't know exactly how; that's up to the Lord. But He will do it."

The next summer I ran into the guy again, and he reported that his marriage was a lot better. What was the difference? He said it was because, in the previous year, Jesus' love had finally flooded his heart.

Pastor Charles Stanley has written: "The essence of the Christian life does not consist of a set of rules and regulations. It is sharing a moment-by-moment, intimate relationship with the Savior. It is not a matter of human acceptance. God accepts us—that is all we need."[1]

Jesus' command to abide in Him (John 15:4) is actually an invitation to live in His presence. As I've welcomed Him into my decision-making process, His presence has become a deeply personal part of my experience, and it is one of my greatest joys. If you are lacking the experience of Jesus' presence, humbly ask Him to make Himself real to you. To pour out His affection on you. To bring you to a point where you are comforted by His presence rather than scared or confused by it.

A sincere request like this, prompted by the Holy Spirit, is one that He will honor. And as your relationship with Christ grows, you'll reap the rewards that Christ lived and died for: "Friendship with the Savior is a continuous unveiling of His love and care for each of us. The life that remains focused on Jesus Christ is a life that enjoys unbroken fellowship. It is a life of victory, peace, hope, security, and most of all, friendship."[2]

My ministry consultant, Lynn Ziegenfuss, is a spiritual director and leadership trainer. She and I have teamed up in the section at the end of this chapter to share some specific suggestions for practicing Christ's presence in your everyday life. This is something you want to absorb into your soul, not just understand intellectually. Anytime you can get His love in your heart, the more you will act out of that love.

What Friends Do

After being overwhelmed with the Lord's love during that beach vacation in San Diego, you can imagine how excited I was when I read Jesus saying to His disciples in John 15:15: "I have called you friends, for everything that I learned from My Father I have made known to you."

Think of what friends do: They're quick to listen. They give you a hand when you need it. They support you and celebrate you and encourage you. They're protective of you. They think of you often. They freely share their own lives with you so your relationship isn't a one-way thing. Most of all, they love you. And they don't just say so; they actively show it by being dependable and going out of their way for you.

By Jesus' own words and actions, He is not only that kind of friend, but He clearly desires such a relationship with each of us.

Once you start thinking of Him as that ideal, ultimate Friend who cares in all those ways, how could you not include Him in your life, and especially consult Him in your decisions? Granted, you don't see His actual face in conversation, yet that doesn't stop the flow of communication in other important relationships. For example, what do you do when you're traveling and want to talk to a loved one? You connect in other ways.

It doesn't have to be any different with Him. He has written out His thoughts and plans, expressed His love, offered His wisdom—all in the words of the Bible. We can read them anytime to learn more of who Jesus is and His dreams for us. We can speak to Him in prayer (which is simply another form of real-time conversation) and journaling, telling Him our concerns, our joys, our hopes. And He does respond in real time—through His Spirit and His Word, through worship and teaching, through our circumstances, and through the love of others. So invest in this relationship. Cultivate your friendship with Jesus. It will make all the difference in your ability to align yourself with Him and receive His answers.

"I spent years and years giving my family my leftovers," said one of my mentees. "I'm a professional at giving that to the Lord too. If I'm really seeking His will, I need relationship. If I can give three hours to a football game or a business meeting, why can't I afford an afternoon with my Creator? The truth is, I can't afford not to!" As you learn to relate to Jesus as your Friend, you may one day naturally find yourself relating to Him as your Best Friend. And the closer you get, the more His love for you will come alive.

No Bad Answers

Not only is He the best Friend you can have, He won't ever give you a bad answer. That's a huge bonus. Human friends know your past. Jesus knows your past and your future—and He has *all* the answers. Personally, this makes me want to involve Him even more.

I do not have all the answers, and I don't always follow the ones I should. But Jesus graciously and patiently supplies every solution via His Holy Spirit. He never fails to give me the right answer, because He knows the Father's will. So when I'm presented with a decision to be made, I remind myself that, as my Friend, He loves me and wants to help me. I recall that I can trust Him to have all the answers. And I remember that He is right by my side, pointing the way to God's best for me.

Speaker and author Annie F. Downs says this about her own journey with the Lord:

> I'm learning to pray, asking God to teach me what it looks like to pray from a place of trust. And I'm thankful that when I don't know what to say, the Holy Spirit does. My heart, His plans, perfect harmony. And because of this, I am convinced . . . that every detail of my life, EVERY DETAIL, is continually woven together by God, creating something—in joy and pain—that is more than I could ask or imagine.[3]

Pray First and Until

One of the real blessings of prayer to me is that I get to talk to my Friend Jesus. I'm particularly excited to do so each time I begin the process of making a decision, for we are setting out on another adventure together.

If Jesus isn't your Friend, if you're not sure you can consult with Him in your decisions, go through this checklist. I ask myself these questions whenever I'm feeling distant from Him. They give me a better idea of how to pray and reconnect:

- Do I know His love?
- Do I feel His love?
- Am I including Him in my day-to-day life?
- Do I really trust Him?

The last thing we need is to shut Jesus out or ignore Him in our decisions. Pastor John Piper gives some much-needed perspective on what we're missing if we fail to draw close to Jesus for His counsel:

> There is a direct correlation between not knowing Jesus well and not asking much from Him. A failure in our prayer life is generally

a failure to know Jesus. "If you knew who was talking to you," [Jesus said to the woman at the well in John 4,] "you would ask Me!" A prayerless Christian is like a bus driver trying alone to push his bus out of a rut because he doesn't know Clark Kent is on board.[4]

Jesus is eager and able to help us on our way. Our divine Companion has promised to faithfully come alongside us through the Holy Spirit when we remember to consult Him.

We seldom know best. It's just a fact. But Jesus always does. And He always cares—even more than we do. So don't hesitate. Anytime you're unsure about what to do, pray first. Instead of worrying. Psalm 37:7–8 reminds us: "Be still before the LORD and wait patiently for him . . . do not fret—it leads only to evil." Worry makes us hurry— and we've already seen the damage that hurry can do.

Also, pray to understand your role. This is one of my primary goals in connecting with Him early on in a situation. It's easy to run ahead with my ideas or to expect Jesus to take care of everything. As partners, however, I want to make sure I'm not asking Him to come down and solve something when I should instead be "rising up" (in heart and in spirit) to see what my role is in the situation at hand. I try to continually ask Him, "What do You have for me to do, Lord?"—all the while paying attention to whatever He seems to be doing in my life and seeking to join Him in it. Doing my part, but staying connected to Jesus every step of the way, goes a long way toward helping me remember He is not some genie in a bottle, operating at my whim; He is my dear Friend who loves me like no one else does and my trusted Partner who knows the best course of action.

Finally, keep praying until you have an answer. This is not just a one-time request every time you face a decision; it's not a one-and-done. Prayer is most effective when it becomes a way of life. So grab some one-on-one time with Him and ask Him what He wants you to do in the current situation—but don't stop there! Pray as you're slowing down. Pray as you're following through. Pray as you obey.

Our prayers to the Friend of all friends is the bridge across which we travel as we seek to get neutral. These ongoing conversations not only span the gap between our ignorance and our obedience of God's will, but they undergird the entire discovery process.

As Oswald Chambers challenged: "Think of the last thing you prayed about—were you devoted to your desire or to God? Determined to get some gift of the Spirit or to get at God? . . . The point of asking is to get to know God better. . . . Keep praying in order to get a perfect understanding of God Himself."[5]

··

Practice His Presence

When you have a daily connection with Jesus as your Friend, a transforming experience of His love is not far behind.

With that said, it is my understanding that for people who have suffered neglect, trauma, or abuse of any kind, it can be especially hard to recognize Jesus' goodness, particularly if you were violated as a child. Trauma often leads to feelings of shame or "I'm not good enough."

If this is what keeps you from Him, spiritual director Lynn Ziegenfuss suggests thinking back to those painful times (preferably with the help of a pastor or Christian counselor) and inviting your Deliverer and Healer into those helpless moments. This can ease the fear and awaken you to His love in ways you may have overlooked.

One exercise she has recommended to me has been to sit with the passages in the Gospels where Jesus calls the children to come near. Put your wounded inner child in that scene and imagine what it would feel like not only to be near Jesus, but for Jesus to take you in His lap and talk with you.

Here are some additional suggestions from Lynn and me that we hope will help you let down your defenses so that Jesus can embrace you in His unlimited love and acceptance.

- *Expect Him. Look for Him. Anticipate Him, just as you do anyone you long to see.* The late preacher and motivational speaker Norman Vincent Peale urged his audiences that, according to Matthew 9:29, they would not receive a blessing from God greater than their expectations.[6] There may be exceptions, but I am convinced that we generally sell the Lord short. To believe that the One who gave up everything to be with us wants to intimately connect with us is far less a leap of faith in my mind than the miracles that we take for granted every day—like hopping on a plane and expecting to arrive safely at a destination several thousand miles away, or trusting that gravity is going to keep us from suddenly launching into outer space. If we can believe things like that, things we don't totally understand or can't physically see, we are capable of trusting that Jesus can—and will—make His presence known to us individually through the work of the Holy Spirit.
- *Ask Jesus to direct your thoughts to this moment and to be in it with you.* Before I became a Christian, I was rarely present to what was going on around me. Instead, I was constantly projecting into the future, envisioning either success or failure. The present, however, is where Jesus lives. That's where you have to be to find Him. When your thoughts begin to wander to the past or the future, confess your distraction as soon as you recognize it, and have the Lord redirect your mind so you can be present to His revealed presence.
- *Treat Him as you would a best friend.* Try calling on Him throughout your day. Approach Him with an open heart, ready

to hear Him, know Him, and include Him in your thoughts, questions, plans, and feelings.

- *Get to know Jesus via the four Gospels of the Bible—Matthew, Mark, Luke, and John.* Their eyewitness accounts of His life on earth have not only introduced Him to people throughout history, but have breathed life into people's perceptions of Christ. You can find Him there as well.

- *Evaluate at the end of each day: "When did I feel Him most present? When did He seem most distant?"* This tunes you in to how much of life you live minus an awareness of His presence—and increasingly sensitizes you to what helps or hinders your experience of His companionship throughout your day. Someone once said, "[God] is found in the middle of the events of your everyday life. Look past the obstacles and find Him." Focusing on what frustrates me or stands in my way will likely cause me to lose sight of Christ. As I focus on Him, however, obstacles start to fall away.

- *Invite Jesus into your worship, your times of waiting, and your work.* He promises in Scripture that when we seek Him with all our hearts, He will be found (Matt. 7:7). The more you consciously welcome Him into these spaces, the more you will sense Him with you through the Holy Spirit.

- *Revisit scenes of Christ's affection for you.* Since we have the ability to envision ourselves doing almost anything—sitting on a beach, hitting a great golf shot, meeting one of our heroes—nothing should be able to hold us back from images of tender moments with Jesus. A few times a year I ask Him to show me His love again, because the neglected little boy in me still needs assurance that he is noticed and loved. I visualize myself as a child, sitting on a bench by the ocean with Jesus holding me on His lap with His arms around me.

- *Develop a grateful mindset.* Those who have no joy naturally feel distant from the Lord. Carry with you a thankful heart, and you'll see the One who loves you more clearly. Pierre Teilhard de Chardin summed it this way: "Joy is the surest sign of the presence of God."[7]

....

CHAPTER 8

STEP 2: GATHER THE FACTS

H AVE YOU EVER KNOWN two people who went through the same experience, sat through the same conversation perhaps, and yet their individual accounts of it were noticeably different? If you're married or you have kids, I'm sure it's happened to you!

I find that, even in the work setting, if we send two people on a sales call, they will each represent the facts very differently afterward. Logically, that means they can't both be 100 percent correct. They aren't trying to mislead anyone or misrepresent what happened. It's just that part of being human means having a hard time absorbing, remembering, and accurately interpreting all the data that comes our way.

Adding to the difficulty is our struggle to distinguish facts from opinions. What if I asked those salespeople to state only the facts of their sales call? Neither of them would ace the test. People are simply too accustomed to regarding opinions as facts, making no distinction between the two.

If all that is true in an everyday scenario such as a sales call, imagine trying to effectively interpret the facts in a situation that involves heightened emotions and desires. I've been practicing this step of my process for a long time, and it's staggering how often I unthinkingly view an opinion as fact, and present it that way to others, only to realize later that it was nothing more than my opinion.

Blind Spots and Biases

This illustrates one of the difficulties of Step 2. Blind spots are a problem here, as are our biases.

We know we have them, so why not just admit it? At least that way we can be more open to the Holy Spirit revealing them at the proper time.

To gather the facts is to do your due diligence for spiritual purposes. I define *facts* in this context as "any data, reality, or truth that could rightly affect a conclusion." One prerequisite for proper fact gathering is the willingness to call things as they are, not as you see them. People commonly treat true facts (actual truth) and perceived facts (opinions or preferences) as one and the same, when in reality these are sometimes polar opposites!

The more dysfunctional a person is, the more filters they'll have for interpreting perceived facts as true facts to fit their paradigm. This is how, before my burnout, I could be gone from my family for days at a time, work hours of overtime week after week, and still claim that my family was my priority.

To receive God's answer, you have to internalize the truth. I've found that thinking out loud with people I trust removes some of my filters so that I hear the truth more accurately. So do prayers for discernment and time spent in God's Word. All of these things force me to ask myself: "Is this my story, or a fact?"

Everybody likes their story; not everybody likes the facts. The upside is that, under the direction of the Holy Spirit, this step can do so much to move you closer to God's will. To gather the facts and prayerfully, properly apply the ones that He reveals as relevant can draw you out of denial, remove your blinders, and shed light on details you've never noticed before. It brings you to the truth of a situation, clarifying which data is worth considering and allowing you to see what you need to see. It also helps you sort through your feelings—what's going on within *you*—so you can get out of your own way. Anytime you can substitute actual facts for perceived facts, you're not only moving in a good direction, you're easing the emotion that almost always accompanies our prejudices.

The truth will set you free, not your opinions. But you really, really have to want God's answer.

Not to Be Ignored

This second step isn't one to be ignored. One of my close friends admits: "As an impulsive person, I tend to want to short-circuit the entire process by just going to the Lord in prayer. When I do this, I take all my biases, emotions, and denial with me—and I don't get a clear answer because of the walls I have. I equate it to getting bad cell service: I can tell my connection's not working. And the reason is because I am leaving out this step. I'm not willing to sift through the garbage and find the truth."

Gathering the facts helps this guy drop his truckload of garbage so that nothing is blocking him from God's will. As he collects and then sorts through the facts, he becomes increasingly aware of what he calls "the truths that can't be refuted" in a situation. They "soak into my soul," he says, "allowing me to see what my flesh doesn't let me see." He exchanges trash for truth—and truth is always at the heart of God's will.

My daughter Tanya says that, for her, gathering the facts allows "the things that pop up from sinful places" to be taken out of the decision-making process. "It shows what's driving me and flushes out my fears." It works for me this way too. Weighing the facts with an open heart and mind makes God's choice more apparent.

Seeking Counsel

The facts include:

1. The unchanging truth of Scripture.
2. The truth of who I am (such as my temperament and talents, my values and principles, and my healthy passions and convictions).
3. The godly counsel of others.

Given what I said at the beginning of this chapter, you may think it odd that I've categorized the counsel of other Christians under the fact-gathering step, because human wisdom is *human* after all. We aren't God, we don't know the future, and we are susceptible to the sway of our opinions and emotions even on our good days. Nevertheless, Scripture clearly affirms the wisdom of having advisors (for example, the book of Proverbs contains many verses on this topic). We just have to be selective about who we look to for advice.

By "selective," I'm not suggesting you choose people who will tell you what you want to hear. You already know what you want to hear, so why would you need a second opinion for that? What I'm referring to are mature, Spirit-filled Christians who revere God's Word and whose lives exhibit faithful obedience to His wisdom. For any decision, you need fellow believers with whom you can talk through all the facts, including any motives and desires that you're aware of, and who will listen with spiritual ears. These people will read between the lines of your life and offer up biblical, emotional, and spiritual truth.

Wise counsel may come to you any moment—not just from people you seek out but from a sermon you hear, a Scripture passage you read, the lyrics of a song on the radio, or an experience someone casually shares at work. The Lord may use the writings or podcasts of pastors, authors, and Bible teachers as well (their messages have certainly had an enormous impact on me). But nothing can substitute for those face-to-face or phone-to-phone conversations with godly friends or mentors who know your tendencies and temptations, and who can call out your gifts and passions.

Sometimes you also need objective "experts" (doctors, bankers, and so on) with proven knowledge and experience in your situation. They may not be Christians, yet all truth is God's truth; thus, even the facts from non-Christians can be used by God to direct you to His will.

These experts aren't always paid professionals. They might be, depending on the type of decision you're making. (For example, if it's a business deal, you certainly want seasoned financial advisors weighing in alongside your personal mentors; if you're considering getting engaged, it makes sense to meet with a marriage counselor as part of your fact-gathering process, in addition to your pastor.) But often the experts are the other moms at your church or that prayer warrior in your neighborhood who seems to know Scripture backward and forward. Regardless, ask the Lord to guide your discernment and their counsel.

In the decision to start Texon and the many, many decisions I've faced since then, the advice of experts and trusted Christians has served to correct my steps, keep me on course, or confirm God's direction. I sought out a pastor for advice in 1987, before I knew whether or not God intended for me to start my own company. This man surmised what was on my heart, saying, "Terry, the only thing that seems to light your fire is business." At another time in the course of that decision, my spiritual mentor—summarizing a quote he'd read—urged me to find out what gives me life and then do it, "because God wants people to come alive."[1] I didn't treat either man's words as being a "Thus saith the Lord," and neither did they. But because their feedback aligned with scriptural principles, it was valid for me to bring their comments to the Lord in prayer.

Valid facts aren't automatically relevant ones. Only God knows what "data" is needed for discerning His will. That's why I take all legitimate information to my Friend Jesus in prayer and then wait on Him: given time, He shows me which is which—what I should keep and what isn't relevant in my current situation.

What About Us?

Now that we've dealt with the handling of other people's input, what about our own? How do we stop ourselves from succumbing to our opinions rather than the truth? After all, our feelings often lie to us, and our preferences constantly clamor for our attention.

Feelings and wants aren't wrong per se, but we must be careful not to regard them more highly than they deserve. If we're not paying attention, they can all too quickly prejudice us in a direction that could be completely opposed to God's will.

Scientists call it confirmation bias, this tendency to interpret new evidence in favor of our preferences. In the fact-gathering phase, it's scary how much we'll discount the realities we don't like and assign additional significance to whatever strengthens our position. But this does not lead to wise choices; in fact, it delays our progress in reaching Step 4 (getting neutral).

The fact-gathering phase is not a time to collect only the information that "furthers your case" for your preferred outcome. In fact, just the opposite! You want to toss into the pile *anything* that might incline you toward a particular choice.

To help me counter my biases, I try to be utterly transparent. To be less than honest with myself, the Lord, or anyone I consult with only delays the time it will take for me to be ready to receive an answer. So while I'm doing my due diligence—working the numbers, evaluating logistics, consulting with experts and wise advisors— I'm also digging deep to uncover whatever fears or selfish ambitions

while the Ten Commandr
mental things God wants

After Tanya has done
facts that are left, "and the
page," she says, "and I sta
finite and clueless about th
supposed to continue in th

While listing pros and
recommends listing your r
comes; but since we can't
Motives are about perspec
He explains, "Have you ne
are usually acting out of ex
devastating shortsightedne
A focus on God—His char
people to wisdom."[2]

In other words, if a m
it out, knowing that it is n
it is wisdom and should b
the data.

Do

Regardless of the decision

I once talked (pushed,
a very large donation to ar
for less than thirty minutes
son, who was very charism
investment this was.

If I had slowed down
learned of the leadership's
weighed Doris's serious co

might be driving me. Reading the Bible and prayer not only help to root out these damaging emotions, but through them, the Holy Spirit examines my heart and reveals what I should be paying attention to. I simply can't discern God's decision if I'm not factoring in what lies beneath the surface.

Until we have the Lord's answer, we are on a journey of discovery. Therefore, I also seek to be as thorough in my fact gathering as the situation warrants, while keeping in mind that I will never have all the facts.

Being persistent with fact gathering in the early stages of a decision is important, as is remaining open to any new facts that the Lord might make known later. But don't get bogged down in the research. We've probably all known people who couldn't act on what seemed an obvious solution because they were paralyzed that more data might be out there. Thankfully, we don't need all the facts on earth to arrive at a decision; only the ones that will guide us toward God's will. Ask the Holy Spirit for peace at the point of *enough*. Confusion is not from the Lord; clarity is His fingerprint.

The Things That Surface

How do we sort through all the facts and opinions in order to let those truths—those decisive factors—surface?

The best way I've found is to do a pro-con list. It's simple. It's objective. It forces you to pause and reflect rather than being impulsive. And it's thorough, letting you get everything out on the table.

I did a pro-con list a couple years ago regarding a property in South Texas I was considering buying. After talking with my wife, my realtor, and a couple of financial advisors, I knew what Doris and I were willing to pay, the current state of the market, and how much comparable properties were going for. I then visited some places, and once I honed in on a particular listing, I got the practical facts about

how well its amenities fit o
want to make, and so forth
and relational pluses and m

- Ways this purchase n
  and people God has c
- My desire to honor m
- What Scripture says a
  possessions, and unde
  approves it
- Whether anything ab
  of my pride (if I'm in
  guests; if purchasing

The answers to these consid
and became data points alo

What's interesting abou
for five or ten minutes after
bubble up—the one or two
resolve. Sometimes you'll c
in a particular area, and tha
soon as I had the potentially
in front of me, the Holy Spi

Once Tanya does her p
that are fear-based or sinful,
helps her confess them to t
deciding factors. If you're u
sus approved by God, com
in Scripture. For example,
obvious acts of the flesh tha
while verses 22–23 feature
provides a further inventory

noticed. Instead, I threw my money in right away—and I had real regrets soon after.

Like most of us, I need some form of accountability to get outside myself, and taking time to gather the facts is one way to do that. Though I've tried the shortcuts, there's just no way around it: you have to move to the slow lane and do your research as the second step on your way to finally getting neutral.

Once you have gathered the facts, the remaining steps of this process seem to fall into place pretty quickly, and you can really start to advance toward the Lord's answer—and the peace that only He can give.

CHAPTER 9

STEP 3: WATCH FOR CIRCUMSTANCES

I DEFINE CIRCUMSTANCES AS "the decisions, actions, or events—typically outside of one's control—that may prove providential in a decision." Whether the data you're considering could be classified as a fact or a circumstance matters less than whether it's potentially important. If it's relevant, I keep it in play, so to speak; if it's not, I take it out of circulation.

How can anyone know what's relevant? You have to watch and pray. Especially regarding this step, time will tell.

Whereas facts are more finite and objective, circumstances require that we pay attention to the unfolding story. You have to let them roll out, with God orchestrating their rhythm, just as a conductor speeds up the tempo or slows it down for emphasis in a song. God may alter or change our circumstances at any time. Sometimes He uses them to guide us to or confirm His answer once we've gotten neutral (Step 4), and sometimes He uses them alongside the facts to help us get neutral.

Either way, let a circumstance play out before you respond to it. See if an event or someone's actions gains "legs" as you stay in step with God. If it does, and you haven't yet received a definitive answer from the Lord, add it to the storehouse of potential data points. With time, the data points that matter will add up—they will tip in a particular direction—giving you a greater sense of God's will.

Curveballs

You've seen how, after my burnout, God guided my steps through the unexpected actions of my business partner, Ken, and later, my boss Bill. He did so again in 2010, when Texon was selling its entire butane blending business. I had received clear peace about putting this division up for sale. But then two circumstantial curveballs were thrown our way. The first was when the initial buyer dropped its purchase offer by 25 percent at 5 p.m. on Christmas Eve, five days before we were supposed to close. To this day, I don't know why God allowed that first deal to fall apart. But being forced to start all over with the second-highest bidder did cause me to give up some of my pride. The second curveball came when our primary customer in that business said they did not want us to sell to that next buyer. Complicating things even further was that the CEO of the buyer said they would probably not pull the trigger on the deal if I took the key customer out of the sale.

This was a new set of circumstances that had to be factored in. We have to be alert to changing circumstances such as these, willing for the Holy Spirit to direct us—and aware that He might even redirect us—through unfolding events.

As I got neutral in light of this new information (Step 4), I grew prepared to heed God's will, whatever it might be. In the end, His solution to this unplanned turn of events wasn't practical by worldly standards, but it turned out to be a wonderful solution: we honored our customer and split the business, keeping our customer's portion and selling the rest.

My collaborator, Kris, has been practicing a version of waiting on the Lord for several years now (though she never spelled out the steps). The first time she really remembers shifting to a sacred pace for a decision was on a car purchase. In that instance it was God's movement in the circumstances, after she had gotten neutral, that led her to a clear answer. I'll let her tell the story in her own words.

About six months after I'd sold my high-mileage car and bought my boss's newer sedan, I came across a sporty six-speed at a dealership that really excited me and got great gas mileage too. Selfishly, I liked the one in the showroom better than my sedan. But my current car had only 80,000 miles on it and was running great, so I couldn't really justify this purchase.

Rather than risk an impulse buy that I might regret, I decided to run the decision by the Lord first. To consciously pause and go to Him with something like this was pretty new to me, but I'd learned two things from the loss of a serious dating relationship a few years earlier:

1. don't trust myself so much when I think I really want something, and
2. don't rush ahead of God.

I had no clue as to how I might recognize His answer, but I very simply asked Him to show me *His* decision—and to confirm it so that I would know the choice was His and not mine. "And give me the faith to say no if that's how You lead," I prayed.

Once I was off the lot, I researched the car a bit more, took my dad with me to test drive it—and kept praying and waiting. Everything was favorable except the money. It was an unnecessary expense.

In time, I arrived at the point where I was "willing for the Lord to say yes or no," which is how I have always described what Terry has coined *getting neutral*. And soon after, I was convinced—not just financially, but also emotionally and spiritually—that I was not supposed to spend that kind of money at that time. So I moved on, a little sad that it didn't happen, but feeling okay with it.

One day about two months later, my car engine cut out unexpectedly on my way to work. I was able to restart it and continue on, but less than an hour after I'd sat down at my desk, building management came looking for me. "Your car caught on fire in the parking lot," the woman reported. "The fire department has put it out, but you need to go out there and retrieve your stuff."

I was dumbfounded! How could a well-maintained car be sitting in a parking lot for thirty minutes and then catch on fire?! But it had.

Once I filed my insurance claim, I nervously waited to hear what the settlement would be. By nature, I'm not an overly trusting person. But more and more, I'd been seeing God's tenderness toward me since the breakup with my boyfriend—and often, that tenderness came in unexpected ways. I felt sure enough about the Lord that, prior to the insurance call, I actually declared to my pastor, "I believe God will take care of me in my singleness, no matter how things end up!" And though that was maybe as much a hopeful statement as a faith statement, I was at least trying to rely on God as my Husband and Provider and Advocate, just as the Bible told me I could.

And then one day, the call came. Friends had warned, "They'll try and rip you off. Expect a lowball offer." But to my relief, insurance paid me more than what I'd paid for the car. I celebrated after getting off the phone, realizing how God's *no* had spared me from wasting my money several weeks earlier. And then I cried, because I felt so specifically heard and cared for.

Step 3: Watch for Circumstances

I soon returned to the dealership with a check in hand for the cash price I was willing to pay. The salesman glanced at the amount, discussed it with his manager, and with only a bit more negotiation, I walked out with the car I thought I had permanently walked away from. And to my delight, I only had to pay half the purchase price out of my own pocket; the insurance money covered the other half.

Now it's almost thirteen years later, and not only has this been the most reliable car I've ever owned, but it's still going strong after 250,000 miles! I've always called it my "God car"—and for good reason: it came direct from His hand. Not because I had to have this particular car to get around in, but because I had something important to learn about trusting His *no* as much as I do His *yes*.

I love how the Lord protected Kris from wasting her hard-earned money, all because she was willing to wait on Him and see things through at His pace.

The Next Step Made Plain

Stories like ours affirm something I have only recently recognized: moving at God's pace means we don't have to overanalyze the facts or the circumstances that come our way. God directs our paths in part by arranging circumstances to reveal and confirm what He wants us to do—and when. He will make the next step plainly known, as long as we're intent on learning His plan. Our job is to watch for His answer, be flexible, and do what He prompts us to do.

What a relief this is! To understand that God does all the heavy lifting when we're faced with tough decisions takes the pressure off. We just have to alter our speed, wait once we've gotten neutral, and then follow His lead, which gets easier and easier as we learn to trust that He sees and knows all the things we don't.

These are the truths I keep coming back to. The truths that constantly encourage me and give me the confidence to seek the Lord's will over my own:

1. He knows best, and I only think I do.
2. He sees the future, and I can't.
3. He loves me and the people around me more than I ever could.

What's more, He promises to not only direct my paths but to guide my steps (Prov. 16:9) so that I receive the desires of my heart—the godly desires God "knit" within me (Ps. 139:13; see also Ps. 103:1–5) by which He will fulfill His unique plans and purposes for me. I rarely know what those desires are in the early stages of a decision, but getting on pace with Him helps me figure them out.

Responsive

How often do you read a devotional or something in the Bible and it proves providential? We need to be open to providence in all its forms, particularly at this step in the process.

George Müller thoroughly believed that we should not only take circumstances into account but consider them providential: "These often plainly indicate God's Will in connection with His Word and Spirit."[1] I agree. Because God sovereignly knows all things and controls all things, every circumstance then either derives from or is allowed by Him—and He uses them in often-surprising ways to show us *His* way. Therefore, I want to not only pay attention to circumstances but accept them as coming from His caring hand, even if at first they feel disappointing. This means being present to circumstances as they arise, letting the Lord redirect me as He sees fit, and making prayerful adjustments in my mind and heart.

Pain and disappointment, surprises and so-called coincidences (which never really are coincidences)—these can all help us more clearly see the circumstances that matter. The surprises might be good ones, such as Secretary Hodel speaking at my church in the pre-Texon days, or they might be painful. Regardless, they are a blessing, because they play such an important role in keeping us on God's schedule, operating at His sacred pace.

I can't ever say what God may have planned for me miles down the road. All I can do is be responsive to the facts and the circumstances in this moment, knowing that He sees the future, He knows best, and He loves me more than I love myself. Once the Lord gives me His peace, I'm confident He will faithfully move me another step in His direction, on toward His desires and purpose for me. So I hold the unfolding plan lightly, because circumstances may shift me—or save me—at any time.

I once made an offer to buy some land for hunting before allowing time for God to answer. I justified my haste by promising myself, "I'll come to the point of peace during the due diligence process," which was extensive. Yet privately I was worried I never would get there because I had already sped ahead of the Lord. The seller and I reached a verbal agreement on the property, but as Doris and I were securing the earnest money in order to sign the purchase agreement, somebody else made a last-minute offer—not for more money, but for a simpler contract. This circumstance was my wake-up call. I decided not to match the offer, knowing deep down I never should have chased the deal without God's go-ahead in the first place.

Though I was disappointed that day, I accepted that this was the Lord's answer. And by the next morning, I was actually relieved, because my emotions had settled enough that I could see my sin in rushing ahead. God had protected me from myself through His hand in my circumstances.

He does that for every son and daughter of His who is paying attention: He either uses the facts and circumstances to save us from ourselves, or to send us another step farther in His intended direction. Either way, we win.

CHAPTER 10

STEP 4: GET NEUTRAL

I KNOW WHAT TYPE A people think when they hear advisories such as "Slow down" and "Wait" applied to their lives. To have to adjust your speed for someone else's decision (even if it's a divine Someone) is not on their agenda. It opposes their inboxes and offends their carefully composed to-do lists. It disrupts their high-speed pursuits of whatever is driving them.

I get it.

My current car has 520 horsepower, and it redlines at 6,000 rpm. As you can imagine, I didn't buy it expecting to tag along behind a pace car like the drivers do before NASCAR races. I envisioned going full throttle on the open road, enjoying the breeze on my face and the surge of the engine in my chest.

When you're traveling in the fast lane, windows down, who wants to think about the opposite? When you're equipped for high speeds, what fun is it to ease off the gas and follow God's timetable or, even more frustrating, sit quietly at the wheel with the engine idling? A sacred pace can seem inefficient, and often Step 4 (get neutral) in particular feels more like a barrier to getting where you want to go.

In fact, it would be easy to view this entire four-step sequence for waiting on the Lord as one big delay on your way to Disney World if not for this one reality: *assuming God's pace—and staying on it through this*

all-important getting neutral point—is essential for discerning God's will.
So whether you're a type A, B, or otherwise, every person needs to learn
to push his or her particular pause button in order to watch and pray.

The Work of Waiting

This fourth step, as much as any part of the process, involves faith.
Because, by nature, waiting to get neutral does not feel active. Neither
does it seem a time when God is at work. To be praying, gathering
facts, and watching for circumstances engages us and offers tangible
forward progress. But waiting? It's not an obvious movement toward
God's will. My hope, however, is that by the end of this chapter you'll
be newly encouraged at all that God does while we're getting neutral,
and you'll be motivated to actively wait on Him for as long as it takes.

Oswald Chambers said, "[God] works where He sends us to
wait."[1] He also said:

> It should be unnecessary to be constantly saying, "Oh Lord, direct
> me in this and in that." Of course He will, and in fact, *He is doing
> it already*! If our everyday decisions are not according to His will,
> He will press through them, bringing restraint to our spirit. Then
> we must be quiet and wait for the direction of His presence.[2]

Once enough information is in for a decision—once you've prayed
through it, consulting your Friend Jesus; gathered the necessary facts;
and paid attention to any relevant circumstances—wait until you've
gotten neutral. Wait until you clearly know in your heart that you
want His will more than your own. That's when God's answer is most
likely to come.

This entire process, and particularly the effort to get neutral,
means allowing time for the Spirit of God to show you the motives
of your heart—the good ones and the bad ones—and how they are

influencing you. If we don't take this time, if we rush and fail to complete all four steps, our impatience will block us from being able to distinguish God's desires from our fleshly ones. But His best is what we're going for.

Jesus has the answers. To hear them requires time with Him and "ears to hear," as He so often said. Waiting on the Lord at this stage helps me discard even the most subtle desires of my flesh and tune in to the deepest desires of my heart. And in this place of careful waiting and listening, Jesus speaks. His Spirit registers His truth, His answer, along with overwhelming confirmation and peace in the deepest part of me, where the worries of the world cannot reach.

Going That Extra Step—or Mile

Following someone else's lead can be tough. Most of us prefer to be in control, see where we're headed, choose our route. But to go so far as to actually get neutral for the sake of discovering where *God* wants to take you? As you can imagine, that one additional step usually represents a journey all its own. For a couple of reasons, it can seem more like going an extra mile than just an extra step.

First, getting neutral is the most challenging place to be. It's the position in which, no matter how hard you hit the gas, no matter how much you rev the engine, you're simply not moving on, at least for the moment. More than any of the other steps leading to a sacred pace, getting neutral feels like going nowhere, though it's actually the only way to reach the destinations God has mapped out for you.

Second, it's quite honestly the toughest place to arrive at in our hearts. We don't just struggle to stop hurrying and decelerate until we've gotten neutral; we struggle to remain undistracted and ignore what other drivers are doing (or want us to do). We also aren't too eager to ask for directions. It pinches our pride. Feels like weakness. And that kind of vulnerability is painful.

Yet when it comes to my relationships, my investments, my company, and any significant life decisions, I now *choose* to slow down and get neutral. I intentionally work hard to downshift my head and heart. At neutral is where I access a different kind of power. A power not my own. A power that makes everything work together.

A Prime Position

The dictionary says *neutral* means, among other things, to be disengaged. Temporarily disconnected from the means of forward motion. A point of inactivity, energy gone to waste. Getting neutral, however, is not being neutral as we know it. You're not separated from your power source; you're not apathetic, indifferent, noncommittal, passive, detached, or disinterested in any way. Rather, you're in a prime position for obtaining the true desires of your heart. Not only that, you find yourself more passionately engaged in decision-making than ever. Once you've come to this point, you're fully connected to the greatest power in the universe. It's where you truly start to engage the will of the One who knows the way to everything you want most.

This is one reason getting neutral is such an emphasis for me. Though it's only one step in getting on pace with God, it's impossible to discover God's will if you do not fight through all the obstacles to reach this critical stage.

Getting neutral is what boosts your faith and advances you toward God's answers just for you. *Neutral* becomes active once you're finally operating at His speed. To actually get neutral connects you to the Lord in a way that nothing else does. Because you're no longer relying on your own resources, you can more easily tap into His. You gain a newfound capacity for better choices in your life and work.

In my life with God, getting neutral means anything but being disengaged and powerless. It actually compels me to activity out of love for Him. It lets me draw on the strength and guidance of His

Spirit and His Word, and in turn, reach solutions that are more creative, effective, and productive. The Reverend Crawford Loritts has said: "I guarantee if you spend your time in the Word of God, and there's an attitude of yieldedness and surrender to those truths, there'll be power in your life that you never . . . thought was available."[3]

Other Ways to Understand Getting Neutral

There are plenty of ways to describe it. Here are just a few:

- Removing yourself and your emotions from a situation
- Getting out of your own way
- Wanting God's answer more than your own
- Walking by faith, not by sight
- Detaching from whatever is influencing you
- Giving up your rights

One mentoree of mine knows he's at that important stage as soon as his attitude becomes, "Option A, B, C, D—all are okay with me." My daughter Jeannie says:

When I'm finally neutral, I feel empty, like a cistern, and then I'm ready for the Lord to fill me with His will. So I go back to Him, and sometimes I say, "I need You to lead, God." Other times I ask Him to carry me so I have the courage to do what He is asking: "I'm willing, but I need Your help." My husband and I always go back to "Lean not on your own understanding." And when we do, we find that, no matter God's will, we can honestly say, "It is well with my soul."

One of my favorite devotional writers, Oswald Chambers, clearly understood getting neutral. He said, "We have to sit loosely to all those things [that we possess]."⁴ Sitting loosely can look to the world like you're wavering and indecisive, when in reality, you're consciously awaiting the Lord's decision. Wavering is going back and forth—an unstable condition. Holding loosely to our plans stands us firmly on the rock of God's faithfulness while He prepares a way for *His* plans for us.

Counterintuitive, Challenging, and Life-Changing

I will admit, this whole idea of downshifting so you can get neutral is counterintuitive. How can such opposing measures advance you on the road to success in business and in life? And how can a process that always involves some pain (because you have to slow down, surrender any ungodly desires, and step out into the unknown) keep you coming back for more?

Yet I can promise you it does—again and again—because these steps take you where you most want to go and deliver you, with fewer detours, to dreams and opportunities you never thought possible. In essence, they shorten the distance to God's will—and give you much, much more of Him! As Janet Erskin Stewart has said: "When you get your own way, you nurse a hideous idol called self. But when you give up your way, you get God."⁵

Is it easy? No. Neither is handling 520 horsepower on a winding road. On the other hand, there's nothing quite as exhilarating as where this ride takes you. It's breathtaking and life-changing all at the same time.

Letting Go

George Müller wrote that 90 percent of our problem is surrendering our will (in other words, getting neutral). He also said that "nine-tenths of [our] difficulties are overcome when our hearts are ready to do . . . [the Lord's] will."[6] It may take a day, a week, or a month or more for me to finally obtain peace over an answer and be ready to do whatever God asks. But if I will slow down and wait, it will happen.

Sometimes I've *almost* gotten neutral, only to falter. Plenty of times we pray and gather facts and respond to new circumstances, but to actually let go of our will, our desire to be in charge, is a challenge. George Whitefield said:

> Before you can speak peace to your heart you must not only be sick of your original and actual sin, but you must be made sick of your righteousness, of all your duties and performances. There must be a deep conviction before you can be brought out of your self-righteousness; it is the last idol taken out of our heart. The pride of our heart will not let us submit to the righteousness of Jesus Christ.[7]

In 2008, our natural gas division was not doing well, and I had become very anxious about what to do. One night early on it was really bothering me, so I got out of bed to process and pray. In the quiet, I sensed the Spirit's clear direction: "Keep the business, but keep it simple." Greatly relieved, I went back to bed. But as time marched on, and the division continued to struggle, I grew tired of waiting and I took things into my own hands—hiring more people, adding more complexity within that division, and spending $2.7 million on software. It was sheer impatience on my part, an ugly failure of trust.

What a mistake! More accurately, what a sin! I was trying to force things, which is never a good thing.

If I'd kept it simple, the entire situation might have been different. But I didn't follow God's instruction, much less park myself and wait for His peaceful answer. My running ahead cost our company a load of money and damaged morale for as long as we owned that division. Every time we tried to implement a new idea, not only did it not work, but things kept getting worse. That entrepreneurial "refusal to quit" is sometimes a blessing and sometimes a curse. In this case, though the Holy Spirit had actually offered me clear direction, I was not willing to listen until I was buried in the mess I'd made. And out of the twelve divisions Texon has started, that's the one failure we've had so far.

Had I taken God's advice three years earlier and done what I was supposed to do, we would've come out ahead. Instead, we sold the division for less money than the cost of the software—and then dumped the software because the buyer didn't even want it!

I think situations such as these are exactly why Archbishop Fenelon challenged us to "never make important decisions in a state of distress. You just are not able to see clearly. When you are calm and collected, you will find the will of God more clearly known. . . . Listen to God and be deaf to yourself. . . . Be open to every alternative that God might suggest."[8]

For somebody who loves speed as much as I do, I can be a slow learner sometimes. Which is why I'm trying to be transparent in this book. I'm hoping that you will get this entire process, right down to its final step of getting neutral, in your soul so that you won't make the mistakes that I have.

Delight and Desires

As a young Christian, Psalm 37:4 absolutely exploded my misconceptions about God: "Delight yourself in the LORD, and he will give you the desires of your heart" (ESV). Hearing that the One who breathed life into my lungs will give me, little ol' Terry Looper, my heart's desires if I will find my joy in Him couldn't have sounded sweeter! Now, though, I understand that what I first interpreted in a self-serving way actually has two very God-centered truths behind it:

1. *I delight in Him best when I want His will most.* If I have no joy, I am distant from God. The first tenet of the Westminster Shorter Catechism is that we were created to glorify God and enjoy Him forever. I believe we delight in the Lord when we genuinely want His will more than our will.

2. *God helps me desire His will if I wait on Him.* Archbishop Fenelon had as his goal, "Fear nothing but to fail God."[9] I may not be at that point in the moment—what appeals to the Lord may not yet appeal to me—but if I remain on God's pace and persevere in getting neutral, He will make His plans plain.

The Reverend Henry Blackaby, in his multimillion-selling book *Experiencing God,* summed up our goal this way: "'What is God's will for my life?' is not the best question to ask. The better inquiry is, 'What is God's will?' . . . Once I know God's will . . . I can adjust my life to Him."[10]

Do you recall what God said to Job? "Pause a moment, Job, and listen; consider the wonderful things God does" (Job 37:14, GNT). The wait opens our eyes *and* our ears.

Waiting until we're neutral, where we want His best over what we presume is best, is exactly what enables us to make the necessary adjustments when we do receive His answer.

If you believe you've gotten neutral but can't seem to find peace from the Lord about whatever decision you're dealing with, then stay on slow and keep repeating the first three steps. God is faithful to respond to every heart that is devoted to Him.

Shutting Off

Fenelon wrote: "Thinking too much will distract you. If you become trapped in your thoughts, they will blow out your inward spiritual sense like a wind blowing out a candle."[11] I've found this to be all too true.

The three steps that lead to getting neutral help keep your spiritual flame burning. Certainly there is intellect involved, especially at the fact-gathering stage where you're getting all your data and consulting with others. But once you have those facts and have prayerfully weighed them along with any relevant circumstances, it's time to quiet yourself and let the Holy Spirit complete His work.

He directs us in innumerable ways: a virtuous thought or phrase or nudging that will not go away until we act on it; a simple, practical instruction; our circumstances or the accumulation of facts, all tipping in the same direction; sometimes a dream, or a conversation, or repeated reminders. I know of Christians who have prayed and prayed about a concern and, in the course of twenty-four hours, the same message has crossed their path in a Bible verse, a song on the radio, a billboard, and a conversation with a stranger. Once I receive God's leading, signaled by an abiding peace in my gut (see sidebar), I try to shut off my mind so I can focus on accepting and acting on the answer rather than seeking to rationalize or explain it.

Eventually there may come a time to explain why this seemed the answer and how it appears to have led to the bigger outcome, but first, get peace that it's right without worrying about the why. The "whys" can make you second-guess what is happening on a supernatural level and send you back to living by sight. They can cause you to start listening to the doubters in your midst when it's a time for faith.

At Peace Within

Someone passed along George Müller's pattern for relinquishing his will several years after I'd been practicing my four-step process, and I have always appreciated his explanation of how he gained peace around an answer. Here is Müller's process, in his own words:

I seek the Will of the Spirit of God through, or in connection with, the Word of God. The Spirit and the Word must be combined. If I look to the Spirit alone without the Word, I lay myself open to great delusions. . . . If the Holy Ghost [Holy Spirit] guides us at all, He will do it according to the Scriptures and never contrary to them.

Next I take into account providential circumstances. These often plainly indicate God's Will in connection with His Word and Spirit.

I ask God in prayer to reveal His Will to me aright.

Thus, through prayer to God, the study of the Word, and reflection, I come to a deliberate judgment according to the best of my ability and knowledge, and if my mind is thus at peace, and continues so after two or three more petitions, I proceed accordingly.[12]

The fact that Müller continued to pray and petition the Lord after arriving at a peaceful resolution is something I try to do as well. I find that the Holy Spirit often confirms the answer somehow (perhaps through circumstances, further prayer, or a word from Scripture or others), probably because, in our humanness, we typically need the reassurance that we're not making things up.

Whereas Müller would proceed if he had peace in his *mind*, I do not proceed until I have peace in my *gut*. According to my scholarly friends, the difference is really more a matter of semantics than Müller or me making a hard distinction between our heads and our hearts. We are both saying: we try to listen intently to what the Spirit might be communicating, how He is leading, and we keep listening until we have assurance and clarity at the core of our being.

The Marks of a Godly Answer

The Bible frequently uses terms such as *body*, *soul*, *spirit*, *heart*, and *mind* interchangeably, and the Spirit of God is capable of speaking (out loud or internally) to any part of us. When I use the word *gut*, this is how I describe the visceral feeling that stirs my insides—body, soul, spirit, heart, and mind in unison—when the Holy Spirit has revealed God's will to me in a specific situation.

The assurance of God's answer is further marked by the clarity with which He guides me: He either delivers a distinct solution or answer, or He prompts me to a definitive idea or course of action. Further, the message will be tangible and applicable and simple, not vague or mystical, and not confusing or complicated. And the deep-seated peace that accompanies it, along with any equipping I might need to act on it, is His fingerprint. That peace will be physical—penetrating my body and soothing me right down to my soul.

Some people like to claim that I'm acting on a hyper-developed intuition most of the time rather than the movement of the Holy Spirit. I will admit, I'm probably more naturally intuitive than most men. In fact, people sometimes tell me, "I don't get feelings in my gut." But I say, "You would if you tried." It's a matter of practice and a willingness to hear beyond the noise. Even more so, if you're a Christian, it's about tuning your frequency to the Holy Spirit so God's voice registers when He does speak. (I'll share more on this in the next chapter.)

Learning to hear the Lord takes practice. But the more you listen—and get to know Who you're listening for—the more quickly you start to recognize when a prompting is from Him. John 10 says that Jesus, our Shepherd, knows His sheep, and His sheep know His voice. If we are His sheep, we will know His voice when we hear it. We will hear it above the noise of the crowd, just as a child can pick out his mom or dad's voice, sight unseen, over other voices in a public place. And the Holy Spirit will make sure we don't miss it.

Unexplainable but True

I often tell people: "You may be skeptical, but this process has worked for me for thirty years. If you sit quietly and eventually turn off the voice of your flesh and of every person who is weighing in, what does your gut say? *That* is what you should do. Not what your flesh, your impulses, say. A person's flesh voices all their sin and insecurities. The answer must be from your gut, with no final influence from anyone else."

The only final influence should be the Lord's. That's what we're striving for: His decision, not ours. The direction you receive from the Holy Spirit may feel like anything but a joyful answer to prayer. In fact, the odds are you won't be thrilled with the answer at first. No one likes to be told no or wait. Yet when you have peace, it is *the* answer—and God will help you accept it. Even more, you will ultimately thank Him for it, because the Lord knows what you yearn for.

What I love about God's mysterious ways is that when we finally open ourselves to His decision, He will have worked in such a way that it will, in the end, be the decision we want too!

You remember how Doris and I were considering buying a property in South Texas? Well, one morning we both got peace about it during our prayer time. The Lord used the facts most of all to put our minds at ease about not buying the place, even though we both thought we wanted it. Doris's priority is people, and this property wasn't low maintenance enough for her to be able to focus her energies on the family and friends who would visit. As for me, I didn't want to spend the money on a place that wasn't well suited to hunting quail. And we were okay with walking away from it.

I've surprised many people over the years with stories such as this—about God's answer both at work and in my personal life. But they have been *His* answers, and I have never been disappointed after the fact. Incidentally, that's another way you know when an answer

heart." I think we all have a certain amount of courage and willingness to go forward in the face of fear. Especially if we have a deep-rooted peace about the decision—and confidence in the One who has patiently, lovingly brought us to it. God supplies that peace. And He will keep doing it, every time you venture to trust Him.

PART 3

LESSONS LEARNED ALONG THE WAY

CHAPTER 11
....

IS IT THE HOLY SPIRIT OR INTUITION?

I'VE PLACED THIS SECTION here, right after the steps, because I know the steps naturally lead to further questions. Before showing how my family, friends, and I apply the steps in specific areas of our lives (Part 4), I thought it would be helpful to address the most common questions now and include some of the practical ways I discipline myself in order to try and stay on pace with God.

I pray that the lessons I've learned along the way will both ease your mind and increase your willingness to take risks, looking to the Lord in your next decision.

Trusting Your Gut

The first question that often arises in follow-up to Step 4 is, "Why should I trust my gut, as you call it, Terry? Isn't it unreliable and subject to irrational feelings and subconscious fears?" That would be true if I were speaking of the kind of intuition the coaches on my favorite televised singing competition, *The Voice*, are continually referring to. However, the power that is at work when we are actively trying to get neutral is far more than a sense or a feeling. It is a supernatural knowing:

- It goes well beyond instinct or what years of experience teach us. It is a heaven-sent wisdom that transcends time and has existed before the foundations of this world were set.
- It is not just human intelligence or common sense or ingenuity. It is an otherworldly work.
- It is not some vague idea from "somewhere out there"; it is specific truth, grounded in the Word of God and delivered to our souls through the One whom God has provided to serve as every Christian's internal Guide and Filter, the Holy Spirit.

The core of your being has been the repository of the Holy Spirit's wisdom for as long as you've been a Christian. Trusting your gut, in my terminology, is trusting the collection of your experiences as you've walked with the Lord. It holds all the things you've learned, all the insights you've gained as you've studied the Bible, prayed, read thoughtful books, listened to sermons, interacted with fellow believers, and practiced the presence of God. Your gut is also where all the factors in a particular decision are stored—everything from the nature of the prayers you've prayed to the facts you've gathered, the counsel you've been given, and the circumstances you've undergone.

Our natural intuition and our years of experience are things that God uses to point us in the right direction, but real clarity—the specific answers we seek at this stage of the process—comes through this Power, this Person, this divine Being. God's Spirit translates the infinite, unfathomable truths of God into words and ideas we can discern and act on.

As one preacher explained: "Faith is the entire person in the right relationship with God through the power of the Spirit of Jesus Christ."[1] Every time someone accepts Christ into his or her heart as

Lord and Savior, the Holy Spirit comes to live inside. Just as every person is born with intuition, every individual who is *born again* is given the Holy Spirit as part of this new birth. Because the Holy Spirit is one with God the Father and Christ the Son (the Spirit is the third person of the Trinity), He knows the deep ways and thoughts of God. He also understands the depths of everything Jesus ever said and is therefore able to interpret and translate and apply Christ's words exactly as we need them, exactly when we need them.

Jesus said of the Holy Spirit:

- "The Advocate, the Holy Spirit, whom the Father will send in my name, will teach you all things and will remind you of everything I have said to you" (John 14:26).
- "When He, the Spirit of truth, has come, He will guide you into all truth . . . whatever He hears He will speak; and He will tell you things to come" (John 16:13, NKJV).

When it's all said and done and you have the "gut answer" signaled by the steadfast peace of God, you may be unable to recount the exact chain of events by which the Holy Spirit brought you to an answer. Yet your gut has the truth of God readily available, and the Holy Spirit knows both where to find it and how to deliver it so that you can clearly recognize God's will for your situation.

Not of This World

John the apostle assured fellow believers that, thanks to God's provision, we each have the spiritual capacity to discern God's truth: "You have been anointed by the Holy One, and you all have knowledge. . . . As his anointing teaches you about everything, and is true, and is no lie—just as it has taught you, abide in him" (1 John 2:20, 27, ESV).

In His multiple roles as divine Helper, Comforter, Power Source, and Mentor, the Holy Spirit communicates heaven's truths and delivers heaven's answers about our lives on earth so that we will know God's will. He then gives us the power to do God's will and supplies the peace that confirms God's will.

With the Spirit living inside us, we never have to wonder what is right or wrong or what is best. He guides the people of God through this life in transcendent and mysterious ways, and yet, He delivers His guidance by such real-world methods that we don't have to fret: every individual who truly wants God's answer will get God's answer. Only be willing to watch and pray, gather information, and wait.

The Spirit makes unique insight available, especially in matters involving obedience and the will of God. What the Holy Spirit reveals through the Bible and in the spirit of all believers is not "the wisdom of this age" but "God's wisdom" (1 Cor. 2:6–7). The apostle Paul explained where this secret wisdom comes from: "The Spirit searches all things, even the deep things of God. . . . No one knows the thoughts of God except the Spirit of God" (1 Cor. 2:10–11).

Paul explained the difference between those who operate by the Spirit's knowledge and those who don't: "The person without the Spirit does not accept the things that come from the Spirit of God but considers them foolishness, and cannot understand them because they are discerned only through the Spirit" (1 Cor. 2:14).

Jesus said that, upon His return to heaven after His resurrection, we could expect two things: God the Father would not only provide "another advocate to help you and be with you forever—the Spirit of truth," but the world would not accept Him "because it neither sees him nor knows him. But you know him, for he lives with you and will be in you" (John 14:16–17). This is why my unconventional decisions, especially in business, have confounded many of my colleagues over the years.

Deciding to start a company on only a forty-hour workweek without any sales goals was foolishness minus "the mind of Christ," which the Spirit provides (1 Cor. 2:16). It could have been career suicide had the answer not been spiritually discerned and spiritually protected. But because the Spirit *is* truth (1 John 5:6), He can communicate nothing except what comes from God. So I could trust His guidance, and you can too.

A Christian is foolish to *not* follow the voice of the Spirit, because the Spirit's answers originate from above. Does this mean we will always listen for that "still, small voice" that Scripture speaks of? No. God's people can, and sometimes do, ignore the Holy Spirit. But if we do, we are discounting the One who aligns us with the desires of God and who helps us discern the voice of God.

Signs of the Spirit

For every Christian, the Holy Spirit is the One who reveals the things we need to know on this earth and who assures us of God's direction even when we can't articulate why we know that we know. And the primary signs of that divine direction are not only a peace that is beyond understanding, beyond circumstances, beyond ourselves, but also outcomes that promote "love, joy, peace, patience, kindness, goodness, faithfulness, gentleness, self-control" (Gal. 5:22–23, esv). This is how we know it's the Spirit of God at work rather than simple human intuition or skill—not only do we gain discernment about God's will, but our character actually undergoes transformation so that our choices and values more closely echo Christ's!

Human intuition either nudges us in a general direction or alerts us when there's danger. In threatening situations, intuition provokes the biological fight-or-flight response we all learned about in school. A non-Christian is wise to follow his or her intuition because it's based in fact—your physical senses are registering that something's not normal, telling you there may be a threat to your safety.

The Spirit works above and beyond our physical senses. He attunes believers to God's answer and evokes an extraordinary peace that enables us to do what God wants, even if we're scared. Presbyterian minister E. Paul Hovey has said, "Jesus promised His followers that 'The Strengthener' would be with them forever. This promise is no lullaby for the faint-hearted. It is a blood transfusion for courageous living."[2] The Spirit actually inclines us to "stay and obey" rather than to "run or resist." To run or resist is our instinctive, human response; to stay and obey is the Christian's Spirit-led response.

The Gut Answer

The gut answer is the God answer if, as a follower of Christ, you're attuned to His Spirit. What's in my gut is what I'm sure of in the morning quiet before I start my day, for example, or maybe in the stillness before I drift off to sleep at night. It's not the pride-driven, impulsive, restless, anxiety-producing things I think all day long.

A friend of mine, Gino, saw this firsthand not long ago. We serve on a camp board together, and Gino's approach to godly discernment in his decision-making is very similar to mine except that he specifically prays for the Lord's wisdom before he goes to bed at night. Many times, as he awakens in the silence the next morning, undisrupted by the noise of other thoughts, God's answer is revealed—Gino receives the peace and clarity he prayed for.

Awhile back, the camp board and the camp management team were seeking how best to use key staff at each location. Obviously, people's lives would be affected, as well as the momentum at the various sites. Lengthy conversations were had. We board members were consulted, and the staff was heard regarding their preferences. Everything was soaked in prayer. And still, the head of the camps— whom we'll call Justin—didn't know what to do because there was valid rationale for each of the options.

In a summary email to all of us about his uncertainty regarding the best answer, Justin listed out the options and the validity of each one, and he concluded with his "newest preference," simply to let us know where his head was so we could continue to pray. Gino offered his advice to Justin via email that evening, advice that differed from the thinking of some of the people on the board, including Justin's.

Though Gino went to bed that night believing the solution was one thing, he prayed for clarity before falling asleep. The next morning, he woke up and knew instantly that the team consensus was right—and that his advice to Justin the previous day was *not* God's answer. And he understood why in a way he hadn't before.

The answer had God's fingerprints all over it:

1. Gino had full peace in spite of the surprise of landing completely contrary to where he'd been in his thinking only hours before.
2. It honored the staff and their marriages as well as the mission of their camps, all of which God had purposed.
3. There was an unexpected, creative element to the solution. Specifically, the answer allowed key people to serve in their areas of giftedness and passion; and, as so often happens, suddenly another name came to Gino's mind—someone who had the background to fill in the operational gaps that would be left in the wake of these personnel shifts.

"None of this was in my head last night," he wrote a group of us at 8 a.m. the next day, "but it's in my heart this morning."[3]

According to Pastor Tim Keller, our minds are "simply clearer spiritually" in the solitude of the morning, especially after we've spent time in Bible reading and prayer. "It's like walking up a mountain to [that place] where you can see the big picture of where you have been and where you are going. It makes it easier to put your fear and pride in perspective and see them for what they are."[4]

Because Gino was listening for God's will over his own, the Holy Spirit could conduct a 180-degree turn in his thinking overnight—with Gino having complete peace in the morning. God's work in Gino's heart not only further confirmed the answer for Justin but enabled the camp leadership to act in one accord, which was a wonderful blessing to the entire team.

Undoubtedly, the Lord's solutions are most easily heard if we are submitted to Him. Once we are open to His will, that seems to be the tipping point when His answers flow our way.

Eyes on the Horizon

In any important decision, we need to keep our eyes on the horizon, because His answer is on the way. We don't know when or how the Spirit will deliver it, but we know He is with us, and we can be confident it's coming. Thus, there's no need to rush ahead of heaven's schedule—you are in the right place, getting neutral, and moving at the right pace. Just wait with an open heart and mind for God to give you His answer.

As one classic writer said it: "Be quiet, and He will soon be heard."[5]

CHAPTER 12
....

WHEN TO SLOW DOWN

S O WHEN SHOULD WE start to slow down and work to reach neutral? Do we need to apply this process to *every* decision, or only the big ones? Certainly the answer to these questions can differ from person to person depending on the circumstances and one's personality.

Four Criteria

Here are the four criteria that most typically apply in my own life—when I need to slow down and intentionally seek out God's sacred pace.

1. I only strive to get neutral on things that really matter to me.

I was recently invited to serve on the board of a prestigious institution that would have allowed me to rub shoulders with men and women I admire. Rather than allowing me to become caught up in the glamour of the opportunity (something my pride often inclines me to do), my mentor cut to the chase by asking me this fundamental question: "Do you feel passionate about it?"

My answer was immediate: "No." As wonderful as their work is, I just wasn't excited about serving on another board.

"Then I think you have the answer," he said. I didn't bother to filter through the four steps in this decision because it didn't deeply inspire my interest in the first place. The leadership of this institution deserves board members who will be enthusiastic about serving on its board, and my heart was not in it.

When there's little risk involved, I find I'm able to align my will with God's pretty easily. It's when pride, greed, or fear kick in that I have to really dig in, take the time, and do the hard work.

2. I need to consult Jesus and get neutral on anything I don't have peace about.

My friends Jackson and Cara saw for themselves what a difference it can make to settle down to a sacred pace and listen when they aren't in agreement. Though this husband and wife now take the time to work through the four steps for all major decisions, they first tried it together for the biggest decision of their married lives.

Not that long ago, these exhaustingly busy entrepreneurs were deadlocked about whether it was time to try for a second baby. Jackson, who had just been promoted to CEO of a national real-estate investment company, felt he was ready for another child in spite of the extra responsibility at work. Cara wasn't. Her first pregnancy had been difficult: almost-daily morning sickness and a baby who suffered from colic. They were living in a small house with barely enough space for one child, let alone two. What's more, the social nonprofit she'd founded—a handcrafted goods business that employs and trains hundreds of women coming out of poverty in America and abroad—was expanding, which meant frequent trips overseas.

Since Jackson was used to bringing his will before the Lord on business decisions, he thought he'd apply the process with this personal decision. He also appealed to Cara: "Would you be willing to do this with me?" And to his surprise, she agreed, even though she'd never attempted it before.

The couple intentionally stepped back from the hurry of their lives and took a long weekend to start to "peel the onion," as Jackson calls it—they each slowed down to pray and think through the many variables and competing emotions to decipher God's will for their family.

Besides praying to let go of her plans so she could be open to the Lord's, Cara talked with a friend about her concerns during a walk that weekend. She explains:

> With our high-speed jobs, I felt Jackson and I just didn't have the space, time, or emotional resources to have another baby. It was an overwhelming thought for me. But I also didn't want to make the decision out of fear.
>
> My friend didn't say much, just spoke mostly of letting go of all the things I was worrying about, and letting God be God. Jackson and I both had to get neutral about our plans. For my husband's part, he had to surrender not just the possibility of another child at the time but acknowledge: *the Lord called me to marry a woman who I knew up front has a vision and a work to do versus being a stay-at-home mom like my mom was.*

Sitting down together at the end of the weekend, the pair found they were already in agreement and at peace over the same answer—but an answer different from what either of them expected: they would not try to prevent a pregnancy, but they also wouldn't take any special measures to improve their chances. As Cara told Jackson, "Let's let the Lord decide; I don't need to control this."

Within two weeks, Cara learned that she was pregnant *and* that her company's luxury product line would be launching in a premier retailer's stores across the country a month after she was due. She said:

> While God didn't slow down our jobs as I thought He would, He provided other small graces in our specific areas of need: a perfect

house for us right away. An au pair with an incredible work ethic who had turned down other families because she was waiting for a Christian family with a faith community . . . and an ideal pregnancy with a baby who sleeps when he's supposed to.

Striving for a sacred pace and working to get neutral means arriving at that quiet, quiet place where you can hear the Lord and respond with confidence because you know it's from Him, even though you may have fears. And its benefit is the peace that comes with knowing *He* has called you to this. If not for Him, I would've felt that I created such chaos in my life by having another child. But I have such peace. And we are using this process to make further decisions when we need to choose between family and work.

3. It's important for me to get neutral whenever I'm overly or instantly enticed by something.

Some opportunities are so appealing on the surface that we think, *I don't need to pray about this. It's an obvious yes!* And yet my mistakes have taught me to be suspicious of these scenarios most of all. We often don't know our true motivations, or even our deepest desires, in a situation until we've eased off the gas pedal. We need time to gather all the facts and let circumstances unfold; to determine if what appears to be true at first glance really is, or if it's just a mirage.

About six months into Texon, we were making enough money to pay most of our overhead, except that I was not receiving a salary. Two crude-oil marketers approached me about leaving their company and coming to work for us. With their customer base and their track record, it was clear they knew how to make money—and that they would make Texon immediately profitable. On the face of it, this was a great opportunity at an opportune time, because both my pride and my pocketbook were ready for a profit. But after processing the decision and ultimately getting neutral, I felt the peace in my gut to not hire them. Their philosophy was "high volume/low margin"—the opposite of Texon's service culture. Premium service quickly becomes compromised in a high-volume environment, and we needed to remain true to the full-service values that the company was built on.

Once I slowed my speed, these are the things that became apparent. And while I literally cried over this decision—eager as I was to see some short-term gains in my first startup—God guided me to the best choice. The marketers and their way of doing business did not fit us.

It was a tough call for me because so much was on the line. The previous company I'd been with was successful, but I was the number-two guy there. Now I was in the hot seat, and it was my money. Still, the lessons of my burnout were vivid; I knew better than to just go after what was sparkling on the surface.

Those lessons proved to be right, because years later, one of these men cost his employer millions of dollars by covering up a bad trade until it was completely out of hand. Had I brought these guys in to Texon, they would've added to our bottom line in the moment, but their business approach could have left us swimming in dangerous waters.

4. I need to come before the Lord and get neutral anytime a decision starts to become complicated.

Jesus' answers were simple: *Love God and love others.* His approach to people was simple: *Do unto others as you would have them do unto you.* And I've learned that simple works today as well. If it's simple, it's usually best.

Keeping life and business as uncomplicated as possible has proven to be crucial for me. Anytime something doesn't look simple, I try not to do it. For example, one of my rules of thumb is that if I can't explain the economics of a potential investment to an eighth grader, I'm not interested in pursuing it.

Let me frame for you what I'm saying so we're speaking the same language:

- *By "simple," I don't necessarily mean "painless."* To the contrary, I've found pain to be the best teacher precisely because it simplifies things, filtering out all the unimportant stuff.
- *Simple doesn't always signify easy.* Something can be hard and simple. Like the butterfly whose wings are strengthened for flight by wrestling its way out of the chrysalis, sometimes the Lord wants me to go through difficulty to help me reach the point where I can be most effective.
- *Simple doesn't mean taking shortcuts or the path of least resistance.* In fact, to keep things simple, you have to be that much more diligent about doing your homework, adhering to your values and priorities, and practicing complete integrity. Deception and laziness only complicate your life.
- *Simple isn't simplistic.* Sometimes *simple* has complex consequences and entails significant risks.

As I've shared, the Lord led me to split Texon's butane business several years ago and only sell a portion of it in order to honor our biggest customer. My management team, my board, and my investment advisor all disagreed with this. Truth is, they more than disagreed; they thought I had lost my mind.

I understood my team's thinking. To receive a third less money on the biggest deal in the history of the company for the sake of one customer *was* crazy. And it would be far more time consuming and stressful for all of us—more negotiations, more legalities, more meetings. For me personally, going against my team and having to trust that the Lord knew best was very painful. Yet it was so clear to me that it was the right thing to do at that time.

By submitting myself to the Lord's will through these four steps, the Holy Spirit cleared away my doubts and all obstacles, and—though I shouldn't have been surprised—God's solution turned out to be a huge blessing to Texon. The part of the business we ended up not selling has since earned profits well in excess of the amount of money we would've received had we sold it.

So, make no mistake: simple can have complexities to it. It may feel risky and very out of the ordinary, but in the Lord's hands, if we will allow time for Him to reveal where all the puzzle pieces go, the final picture will be straightforward. Clear. Honest. Purposeful. Honoring of God and others. No nonsense. Right and good.

Simple is a huge indicator for me of the Lord's leading, because in my experience, God likes simple.

Friends of mine in Oklahoma kept simple in their sights for five years as they evaluated a ministry opportunity. This husband and wife believed God had put on their heart to make a free place of retreat available for people in ministry rather than turning it into a rental. From 2011 to 2016, they consistently searched properties online and then spent occasional weekends touring properties before God made possible—against some pretty significant odds—a quiet cabin on a lake.

After touring this cabin, they hoped it was the one, but neither of them knew for sure. So they earnestly prayed that God would close and open doors as needed so that the Lord's will would be clear. One morning, a single phrase was on the wife's mind when she woke up: "No extreme measures." The husband agreed that this summed up his desire as well. My friends then drafted an email to both the realtor and the mortgage broker and told them up front: "No extreme measures." They then explained, "If the financing or anything about the deal gets complicated—meaning, we're having to force something to make it work or you're going beyond the normal scope of your job—then it's a no and we're willing to walk away."

This couple was primed to seek simple because the first offer they'd made on a cabin in 2011 had seemed perfect too—a hilltop view overlooking a large river, enough space to sleep several guests, and well cared for. But once negotiations started, things grew complicated. The biggest source of confusion? The sellers kept changing what was included in the price. They claimed on their listing that all the furniture was for sale. Then, in their counteroffer, they didn't want to sell specific pieces of bedroom furniture. On another go-round, they were willing to include the washer and dryer but not the refrigerator—and the little outdoor shed wasn't part of the sale either.

When my friends couldn't get a straight answer after three attempts, they pulled their offer. They were disappointed to walk away because they had really been able to see themselves and their guests enjoying that space. But in obeying the answer they received after slowing down and getting neutral, they were able to do the hard thing. And though it was another four years before they purchased their cabin—a cabin, by the way, that hadn't even been built when the two of them were touring the hilltop place—what God provided for them was what they'd been envisioning all along.

Admittedly, the problem with buying anything is that "more stuff" can quickly become "too much." And when it does, the blessing becomes a complication and a burden. That's why it's critical to submit our plans and purchases, big or small, to the Lord and wait for His peace. I peacefully decline opportunities all the time—including business opportunities—not because my faith is greater than anyone else's but because I trust that, as long as I've slowed down to listen to Him, God will protect me from over complication with a *no* or a *wait* whenever I need it.

If it's a *go*, He will do as He did for my friends and clear the decks logistically, providing everything necessary to make it happen. God's answers don't get much more obvious than that: you have an almost superhuman peace—and you don't have to force a thing.

Aligned Before You Act

I understand one of the reasons people don't want to go so far as to get neutral is because they're afraid God will make them do something uncomfortable, such as sell all their possessions and become missionaries. Cara was concerned that she would have to give up her thriving career at a time when all her efforts were ready to burst into the stratosphere. I still fall back into that mindset myself sometimes. But through the steps of this process, you have the chance to align yourself with God before you act. Then you're not being forced—you *want* to be responsive to Him! And when you are, you'll receive the desires of your heart; it just may not be what's apparent to your heart *today.*

Slowing down to a different pace brought my hidden concerns about the crude-oil marketers into the open, and with that recognition came two things I always sought for in my life but couldn't produce on my own: peace—and the courage—to say no. On a more far-reaching scale, once I got neutral, God honored my surrender of a surface desire (the lust for a quick profit) to gift me with the real desire of my heart, which in this instance was to preserve Texon's corporate integrity and protect my company and employees.

Jackson and Cara, and my friends in Oklahoma, saw similar results. And they, too, discovered and received the desires of their hearts as they reduced their speed and sought the Lord's answer in their situations.

At the end of the day, each of us has to believe in our soul that God delivers what's best. We also have to come to grips with the fact that, in most cases, we just don't know exactly what that is. But He does. And He will be faithful to help us discern it and do it, if we will only ease into a slower lane and listen for Him.

CHAPTER 13

HOW CAN I HELP MYSELF STOP THE HURRYING?

I F YOU'RE ABLE TO get this process in your soul day to day—remaining at a slower pace until you've completed all four steps with every decision that matters to you—you will find that sometimes you won't even be consciously thinking about a particular step, but then something miraculous will happen: you'll experience a real peace in your gut that you can't explain, and you'll know you're no longer operating on your wisdom alone but following a divine prompting.

The simple result that I keep coming back to is this: once you've gotten neutral and you have the peace of God's answer, go with your gut:

- Go with your gut over some economic or business model.
- Go with your gut over what others may have advised you.
- Go with your gut over what everyone else does.

In the same vein, don't go forward if your gut is nagging you that something isn't right.

I believe God most often reveals Himself to us when we are listening to Him, and I've found that hearing Him is easiest when we're proceeding at His pace. As soon as He does reveal His will, to not trust your gut is a mistake. Don't be afraid to go with your gut if, after all that prayer and honest processing, you have peace there. It is very accurate once you've worked through the first three steps of this process to actually get neutral.

What isn't accurate, however, are the complaints that come from our flesh—our sinful nature or selfish self. Archbishop Fenelon cautioned us to trust these complaints "as some people treat their spoiled appetites. Do not listen to them and act as if you did not feel them."[1] There's still a lot of "self" to get rid of, even after you become a Christian. I know this as well as anybody. So something has to be done to counteract those impulses.

I started disciplining myself—doing the opposite of culture and the opposite of my old self—so the Holy Spirit could have time to work through me. Installing the distancing tactics and delay tactics I'll discuss below has helped me resist my personal pressure points, where I'm most prone to the world's influence, and stay on pace with God. These things produce miniature pain (squashing one's pride *does* hurt a little), but the discomfort is necessary if I truly want the Lord's best.

My Distancing Tactics

Because I've learned I can almost never trust that my immediate impulses and inclinations are godly ones, I'm constantly on the lookout for ways to distance myself from the pull of my own flesh and that of the world. The Holy Spirit, concerned that I protect myself from my people-pleasing tendencies, has helped me with different ideas to counteract my flesh. Here are two of my habitual go-tos.

1. Do differently than the crowd.

In general, if you want to do the Lord's will, you'll have to go against cultural trends.

To complete the four steps of the process and ultimately get neutral sometimes means giving up your "I want what I want" ways. You also, however, have to give up the ways of the world. I tend to lump the two together because so much of me *is* the world. I defy my old self by trying to do the opposite of culture day in and day out. Usually if culture's attached to it, it's not of God. So, if I observe others heading collectively in one direction, I typically try to set my sights in an alternate direction unless the Lord tells me otherwise.

Dying to self is half the equation, but you also have to die to the world. Matthew Henry summed up Romans 12:2—and God's ongoing work in our lives—in this way:

> The progress of sanctification, dying to sin more and more, and living to righteousness more and more, is the carrying on of this renewing work, till it is perfected in glory. The great enemy to this renewal is, conformity to this world. . . . The work of the Holy Ghost first begins in the understanding, and is carried on to the will, affections, and conversation, till there is a change of the whole man into the likeness of God. . . . Thus, to be godly, is to give up ourselves to God.[2]

2. Work hard *not* to impress.

I'm not advocating laziness here. As Christians, we are called to excellence in everything we do. I'm saying that, in situations where I know I would normally want to impress somebody, those are the times I need to go out of my way to *not* try to impress them.

For example, I now simply decline invitations rather than explaining why. To respond, "I can't do dinner with you on Friday because I have a meeting with a huge client," or, "I'm taking my wife on a date" can so easily be a backdoor way of saying, "Look at me—I'm important!" or "I'm such a devoted husband." Better to just say,

"Thank you, but let's schedule for a different evening. I already have a commitment."

Going Too Fast

My family and I love to ski. To be gliding along the snow is a wonderful feeling—until you lean too far over the front of your skis. Then you start going downhill too fast and you lose your balance. It's the same with our decisions. If we're moving too fast, and if we refuse to hit the brakes, we can get ahead of God and run ourselves into trouble.

I went too fast one time when I wanted to hire an investment advisor. He was an Ivy League grad and a fine Christian man whom I'd been mentoring. He'd already said he would love to help me oversee my personal and ministry investments. However, he lived several hours away and couldn't make the move to Houston during that season of his life.

Although I had determined that this hire needed to be onsite to do the work effectively, I was rather infatuated with the idea of having someone as talented as him on board. I didn't want to seek the Lord and potentially have to delay my decision; I just wanted what I wanted. Meanwhile, Doris and an employee of our family office kept querying me about the decision. I was so invested in my emotions that I discounted their concerns, valid as they were, and tried to write them off as "My staff's just afraid that I might hire someone to oversee them." But in time, their persistence helped me see that I was again speeding ahead of the Lord. Once I slowed down and sought God's answer, I declined to hire this young man, and he went on to another venture where he has been hugely successful.

God uses my four-step process to help me slow my rate of speed to His. It helps me put the brakes on myself so I don't jeopardize myself or others. This self-imposed delay also has these advantages:

- *It counteracts my sin.* I'm most prone to the influence of sin when I'm in a rush. So the bigger the situation, the greater my need to decelerate. Satan is always looking for an opportunity. He likes to tempt us wherever we are most vulnerable. When we take the time to consider consequences and intentionally combat our impulses, sin is stopped in its tracks and the enemy usually withdraws, preferring an easier target.
- *I'm less likely to people-please or to be manipulated by others.* Choosing a sacred pace before I decide anything important gives me a chance to examine which feelings may be driving me. This clarity strengthens my resolve to follow through on whatever God says, even when others block my path or are trying to pressure me to hurry things along.
- *You'll be a safer person—for yourself and everyone around you.* You don't have to be a NASCAR driver to know that when you go too fast, you risk losing control. You risk running into things, running over things. People can get hurt. Learn to view the slower speed of God as a safety zone that prevents you from racing ahead of Him and causing a lot of damage due to foolish decisions.

If the goal is to become whole—to rise above our worst instincts and enjoy the blessings of wiser decisions and healthier relationships—then we usually have to do the opposite of our inclinations. We tend to make choices out of our emptiness. Therefore, when we're offered some impressive opportunity, our first reaction is all too often our "flesh reaction" (arising from our sinful nature) because our unwholeness has flared up.

Slowing down and delaying your answer diminishes the intensity of your flesh and pride and reduces the likelihood of acting impulsively. This gives you some breathing room, where you can own up to those harmful emotions that are at work and pursue more mature, God-directed choices.

My Delay Tactics

In just about everything, slowing down to a godlier speed is so different from the "now" that our world and our flesh want us to live in. God is eternally patient and concerned about things that last. Most of the time, we are not. So, anything we can do to stop the haste of our lives, silence the conflict of our emotions, and hit pause is a move in the right direction.

I work hard to delay my decisions so I can get out of the Lord's way. The good news is that, as a Christian, I have the Holy Spirit to help me. These practical ideas, along with any others the Lord might give you, will help you enjoy life, be more successful, and achieve the amazing results that come with reaching a sacred pace—and staying there—until you've been led to His answer.

Much of what I'm describing in this decision-making process requires time—time to work through the steps, time to get neutral, and time to wait for God to reveal His will. Certainly there are occasions when a crisis comes up or a circumstance carries a short deadline, and I have to decide sooner rather than later. If I'm forced to say yes or no before I've had clear direction from the Lord, and I feel any consternation, I pass. If there's no anxiety bubbling up, I'll go forward, though I try to keep the brakes on and only inch ahead. Whenever I can control the deadline, though, I give myself ample time.

For all the situations where there *isn't* a rush, here are my best delay tactics—the ones I use all the time. These help me to deflect any artificial pressure to decide more quickly than I should, whether that pressure is due to my own impatience or other people's.

Pray and wait at least twenty-four hours before:

- *Responding to a significant request.* To slow down and wait a full day to carefully evaluate a request is important because my pride can surface at surprising times. It's even raised its ugly head at invitations to serve my church! I need time to align my heart with God's before giving an answer. If I delay my answer even overnight, I have a much better chance of reaching the right decision.

    Will playing golf be honoring to my wife? Will meeting with so-and-so wear me out? Should I take that trip? Speak at that luncheon? Volunteer for that project? Most times, I really can't be sure in the moment. By the next day, though, I usually have better perspective. If I answer too quickly, it might be with the wrong agenda—because I'm excited that somebody noticed me, or because I want to please you—and these things could override my best judgment. If I wait until tomorrow, I am often amazed at my newfound objectivity. (Also, I resort to, "Let me ask my wife." It not only buys me time, but Doris is usually less likely to be caught up in any allure that might ensnare me.)

    There's an ability to see clearly tomorrow that I won't have until then. The objectivity I obtain overnight is a remarkable provision from the Lord.

- *Sending a difficult email.* Waiting until the next morning helps me keep my emotions from getting the best of me. For me to respond in the heat of the moment will almost always be a disaster. But if I wait until the next day, the Lord has time to settle me down, and then maybe that person and I can have a constructive conversation. This way, too, I can make sure I'm not reacting to the speck of sawdust in someone else's eye because of the two-by-four of unfinished business in my own eye.

    On the face of it, this seems to go against the Bible verse that says, "Do not let the sun go down while you are still angry"

(Eph. 4:26), but from what I see across the scope of Scripture, if you commit to dealing with the upsetting situation *as soon as* the emotions are gone (which will hopefully be within twenty-four hours), then you are honoring the spirit of this verse. Many of us tend to either bury our anger because we don't want to have uncomfortable conversations, or we react without considering the damage we could do. You can't have true peace either way. Timing is critical. So do what you must to reach God's pace and get neutral before you confront. But do speak up as soon as your emotions have subsided.

Wait at least a week before:

- *Doing anything with a "great" new idea that comes to mind.* Unlike all the other categories, I don't immediately pray about these ideas. Instead, I write down my brainstorm—and then ignore it completely. For seven days I don't look at that piece of paper, don't think about it, don't show it to anyone else. A week later I review it to see if it's still "great." Most of the time it is not. That's a big lesson in "lean not on your own understanding." I've even had times when, because I scribbled my thoughts in such a hurry, I couldn't read the idea when I came back to it! (That's funny *and* pathetic, isn't it?)

  With enough of these experiences, it quickly becomes clear that most ideas are not from the Lord. However, if it's God's idea, it will still be great a week from now—and then I can start to process through it with Him. If it's forgettable, then thank God He kept me from moving forward!

  To think of all the time and money I've saved my company, my family, and my team by not instantly acting on every "great" idea that comes to mind makes it totally worthwhile. It has also spared me a lot of embarrassment and pain.

Wait at least a year after:

- *Any life-changing event before making any related decisions.* When you lose a spouse, for example, it's best to wait at least a year, if possible, to sell a house or begin dating again. By then, your grief and emotions have had a chance to settle down a little, and you can see more clearly.
- *Any material increase in your income before making any further moves or large purchases.* Receiving an inheritance, a sizable tax return, or a bonus at work often produces an extra layer of temptation to spend. If I've just sold a business, I try not to buy, sell, or change anything of value for twelve months, because it seems to take that long for me to get my emotions—and especially my pride—in check. To delay and ask God before spending that money serves to counteract our sin and selfish desire and actually equip us to make wiser decisions with the funds.

A watch I bought a few years ago is a good example of this principle. Texon had sold its crude-oil division only months earlier. Since I am a deal junkie, I was still on a high from the adrenaline of this transaction. To celebrate, I bought a watch that I thought, by the looks of it in the magazine, would be perfect for me.

I rationalized to myself, *It's just a watch; it's not worth waiting a year for.* But it was. In retrospect, while it was a small thing, I should have held off as the Lord has taught me to do, because my flesh was talking.

To this day, I regret my impulsiveness every time I look at that watch. Because I bought it, though, I wear the watch most days (when it's not in the shop being fixed, that is). To everyone else, it is a nice watch—but only a watch. To me, the prick of pain I feel when I see it on my wrist is a daily reminder of what happens when I don't take the time to get on God's pace.

Here's one more important strategy Doris and I have put into practice:

- *Never decide to buy while you're in the "showroom."* Let's say you're considering some real estate. When you're overlooking the land or standing in the living room of that house, imagining what it would be like to live there, that is *not* the time to say yes. It's too romantic. You have to get out of the "seductive" environment to be able to make good decisions.

  Likewise for any major purchase. Don't decide on a car, a boat, or a motorcycle while you're sitting in the driver's seat. Don't buy expensive jewelry or electronic equipment while it's staring at you in the store or in expanded view on your computer screen. Get away from the time and place when you are presented with a glowing offer: Walk out the door, go home, eat dinner, pray for wisdom—and then opt not to think about it till tomorrow. Do your chores, play with your kids, sleep on it, go to work the next day, run your errands—and then see if some of the allure is gone. You may need to repeat this process for several days or weeks in a row before you know for sure. Just don't buy at first sight. And don't buy until/unless you have full peace in your gut. The showroom is for selling, not for deciding.

Sweet Spot

I think most of us know where we're not whole. We know that when we are overly emotional, our decision to indulge those emotions is likely to keep us from becoming all we're meant to be in Christ. To wait twenty-four hours or a week or a year to decide is a small price to pay. It's a way to be whole in the moment—more like Jesus in a particular situation—despite the fact that we're never completely whole in this life. What's more, God uses the slow-downs and distancing and delays to help us work through particular sins.

Waiting until tomorrow, waiting a week, waiting until the emotions have died down—these are all protections He has provided so that we can distinguish between the desires of our heart and the desires of our head, enjoying the life He intends for His children.

Getting neutral before making important decisions doesn't mean you're more spiritual or less sinful than anyone else—only that God has empowered you to check your sinful passions at the door to want His will more than yours. He is fully invested in seeing that we overcome our old habits and do what we must to get to that sweet, sweet spot of total dependence on Him.

CHAPTER 14

PAIN IS NOT THE ENEMY

O NE OF THE BLESSINGS of decision-making on a sacred pace is that there's a definite end in sight—an answer awaits you somewhere down the road. Plus, you receive the gifts that your Father in heaven wants to bless you with. Yet I would be doing a disservice if I didn't also speak to how painful this process often is. Most of the best things in life are painful to some degree. But the struggle makes the victory that much greater.

Why do we exercise three to four times a week or stay married when we're fighting with our spouse? Because we realize that pain has its benefits—we are healthier, stronger, closer to others for the effort. In getting neutral as in the rest of life: no pain, no gain!

To accept that pain can be a blessing was a lasting lesson from my burnout and something that is absolutely essential to opening yourself to the Lord's will. I know in my soul that I won't usually get more whole without pain. On some level, I think we all know it in our heads, but pushing to get this conviction deep within, where God can change us? That's the challenge.

You don't typically learn your true feelings and deepest desires just because you want to; they are revealed once you've faced the truths you tend to hide from. Especially if you push the limits like I did for so long, you may sometimes have to soak in your pain for a while before God retrieves you from those waters. Thankfully, He really does only allow as much struggle as is necessary to bring us to the place of surrender, the place of peace and clarity that we most long for—and which abiding by a sacred pace allows us to reach.

The Secret Things of God

The Bible says, "The mind governed by the flesh is death"; it is "hostile to God." Thus, "those who are in the realm of the flesh cannot please God" (Rom. 8:6–8). The "acts of the flesh" that keep us from God's greatest gifts include not just sexual immorality and drunkenness, but "hatred, discord, jealousy, fits of rage, selfish ambition, dissensions, factions and envy" (Gal. 5:19–21). Elsewhere, Scripture describes those deathly desires as "the lust of the flesh, the lust of the eyes, and the pride of life" (1 John 2:16).

So is it any surprise that greed, pride, and fear are what pressure us when we're letting our flesh have the final say? Frankly, that's where most of us spend most of our time as people born with a sin nature. But there's another voice inside of anyone who has received a new nature through Jesus Christ. It's the voice of the Spirit of God—and He rarely shouts. His voice resonates in our deepest self, and He has one theme: to reveal the heart and will and mind of God, so that you experience the abundant life and peace that Jesus promised those who are devoted to Him (Rom. 8:6).

Human nature is to run with the answer we can explain, to go with the loud voice of consensus versus the lone whisper within, and to speed ahead with the solution that makes sense to our minds, our training, our background and experience (in other words, our "understanding"). "Don't listen to your self-nature," wrote Archbishop Fenelon. "Self-love whispers in one ear and God whispers in the other. The first is restless, bold, eager, and reckless. The other is simple, peaceful, and speaks but a few words in a mild, gentle voice."[1]

This is a very profound truth, but it is also essential to ultimately discerning what God wants you to do: if you starve the lust of the flesh, your heart will start yearning to be satisfied. *That* yearning is your true desire—and God's delight. That's what you want to lock into and figure out. And that's exactly what the Spirit wants to show you and reward you with if you will be patient and let Him do what He does best.

But you have to make a conscious decision: will you feed your greed or the desires of God?

Like a hungry infant, our greed will always take whatever it can get—it just wants to be fed. And if we feed it and wait five minutes, it will either want more, or it will demand something different to make it happy. When our heart's desires are met, we are truly satisfied, and the contentment lasts.

Know Who Your Friends Are

Once I burned out, the number-one thing that allowed me to grow was the discomfort I'd tried so hard to avoid—pain. A lot of people fear pain when, more often than not, we have pain because of fear. Truth be told, fear is the enemy we need to slay, not pain.

Therapy itself was a lot of pain—but it wasn't as agonizing as the way I'd been living my life. That one fact has trained me to go on the offensive and attack my dragons (my fears) before they attack me. Whenever I need to slay this beast, I try to remember that a dragon is never as bad as we think. So much of it is hollow, a façade with no substance, an ugly face. As soon as I've jabbed at my fear a few times with the sword of truth (the words of the Bible), it shrivels up like a punctured balloon. And that's when I see: there's no need to bail out of my internal pain; it's actually a friend that I should try to embrace.

While pain is your friend, sin is not. But oh, how it seems to be! By that I mean, sin has been a companion my whole life—a tagalong who has served my selfish purposes and supported my every whim and insecurity. But once I realize this is a dysfunctional relationship, one that is actually hurting me, I can start to step back.

Let me repeat: sin deceptively *seems* your friend, but pain actually is your friend. The operating room isn't a fun place, but every time you go through another procedure, your condition should get better; you're a little less sick. When I gave up drinking for a year and a half—just in case I was an alcoholic—boy, did it hurt initially! Same with ending my bond with materialism. In both instances it felt like I was giving up an old friend. And in many ways, I was. An old friend who was toxic and dysfunctional, to be sure, but still a companion and always available.

As we mature, though, that "friend" we used to party with can become a drain—someone we no longer enjoy so much because our values have changed. And as I get some distance from the relationship, I see how destructive it has been. I'm ready to move on; I don't want us to be associated anymore. At that point, when I'm finally ready to turn loose of this relationship, the Lord will take away the pull of that friend to the degree I surrender. His role is to take it away; it's mine to surrender. I will grieve this loss because my sin has been so much a part of my life, but the more I grieve, the cleaner the break will eventually be.

The only way this happens, however, is if I am surrendering my will. No process works if we don't yearn to truly give up our old ways for better ones.

As we choose to listen, the Lord will speak in the pain of surrender. Three years after I sold half of Texon to a Detroit utility, the buyer exercised its option to purchase the other half. During the negotiations, my contact at the utility quit. His replacement did not want to buy all of Texon, and so we decided to sell our crude-oil division to a third party. I immediately found a buyer and negotiated for almost a year—but I had forgotten to seek God's direction. (Yes, I should've known better. But you can see from this example that I'm still very much a work in progress.) Once I finally did get neutral, I strongly sensed in my gut that I was not supposed to sell. I respectfully discontinued the negotiations, but it cost me a year of my life, which was such a waste—and completely avoidable—if I had aligned my steps with God's in the beginning.

We sold that division ten years later for eight times more money. But the main thing, in retrospect, was not the money. I believe God did not want me to sell initially because He had unfinished business in me that could only be accomplished through pain.

Yes, pain.

I do believe God sometimes lets us have our momentary desires, even though they will produce pain, because we will be better off by being miserable for a time and growing through the experience. Either way, it makes me think of this little-known Francois Fenelon quote: "Slowly you will learn all the troubles in your life . . . are really cures to the poison of your old nature. Learn to bear these sufferings in patience and in meekness."[2] Fenelon also remarked, "I agonize and cry when the cross is working within me, but when it is over, I look back in admiration for what God has accomplished."[3]

To process through the four steps enables our fear and pride and selfishness to "be named, surrendered, and nailed to the cross," as my daughter Tanya says it. We are shown where "the fear of man"—that pull toward peer pressure or people-pleasing—may be moving us, or where our pride is getting in the way. Practicing decision-making at a slower pace allows us to admit, "Lord I *am* afraid of what people will think. So I'm going to surrender this and try to hear what you think."

Going through the pain also reveals what your personal red flags are—the things you thought you'd healed from, the things that send you back to your Bible, your pad of paper, back to your knees to refocus on the Lord's will rather than your own.

Pain is unavoidable. You can try and skim by it, but you actually set yourself up for even more of it when you take that approach. I'm not pain-avoidant like I was in my twenties and thirties, yet even after all these years of practicing these four steps over and over, I do sometimes forget how deliberate you must be to reach the place of peace in your gut. Anytime I go through the process on a major decision, I'm reminded again.

With this chapter especially, I want us all to recognize the positives of pain rather than running from it. To focus on the gains—to keep my eyes on the prize—is key for me, particularly when I'm in the middle of the fight. Though everybody's battles are different, I've never gone through difficulty and struggle and not come out better for it. The process of slowing down to a sacred pace until we've gotten neutral may not be painless, but it is very effective. And it comes with a peaceful conclusion. If you want to know God's will, be willing to do what it takes. Even if it means giving up some old friends and finding some new ones.

CHAPTER 15

·························

ARE THEY GOD'S
DESIRES OR MINE?

S O FAR I'VE TRIED to provide in-depth understanding regarding the four steps I use to discern God's will, along with some ideas that can help keep you at a pace where the Spirit's voice can be most clearly heard. In this chapter, we will look at another way of understanding how the Holy Spirit uses this decision-making process. I also want to explore in more detail one of the most common questions that arise when people are trying to apply this process: how do I distinguish between my desires and God's? How do I tap in to my true heart's desires—the ones that lead me to His best for me?

As we've discussed, once the Holy Spirit is dwelling within your heart, you have more than mere human intuition and know-how to help you make decisions. As the Spirit guides you through the four steps, He takes this mix of diverse ingredients that impact a decision and sifts through them to deliver a customized recipe for discerning the will of God in a situation.

Still, if you don't train yourself to wait on the Lord and find out what is in your heart, your flesh can sorely mislead you. If you insist on getting quick answers, seeing your own agenda fulfilled, or gaining what the world has to give, you may have some measure of earthly success as I did—but you'll also have to endure the even greater emptiness and disenchantment that comes with it. And you will never, ever be deep-in-your-heart happy, because you will have missed out on what you wanted the most.

Defaulting to Delight

My default and foundation is a verse that should be familiar to you by now—Psalm 37:4, "Delight yourself in the Lord, and he will give you the desires of your heart" (esv).

What does delighting in the Lord look like? My spiritual mentor and I debate this. He is afraid for Christians to take this at face value because the desires of our hearts aren't always pure. But my contention is that if I'm truly delighting in the Lord—finding joy in what pleases Him and pursuing His priorities—then what I ultimately desire in my heart of hearts, what I want most in this life, will be the same as whatever He blesses me with.

James 4:3 tells us that when we ask things of God and do not receive them, it is "because you ask with wrong motives, that you may spend what you get on your pleasures." The four steps are one way He enlightens us about our greatest desires—which are His desires for us—and ensures that we receive them.

I'm thankful that the Lord doesn't grant us every lesser desire. If He gave us every want that ever enters our minds, we would remain endlessly distracted by small things and never get to the great stuff He has planned!

My pre-burnout goal to become a millionaire is a prime example. I thought for so long that this was the desire of my heart. Clearly, though, having the money in hand didn't satisfy me. If anything, it slapped me with the emptiness of my priorities. Once I became a Christian and could look at my life through the lens of the Spirit, I understood that my desire for money had been a surface "want." It was my flesh talking. What I really craved was acceptance and love and a peaceful mind. I'd chosen wealth and accomplishment as my driving lanes, believing they would be the express route to happiness. Turns out, though, those fast lanes weren't taking me somewhere great; they were just endlessly looping me around a meaningless track. I would have saved myself a lot of trouble if I'd followed Matthew Henry's advice: "Take heed of forming plans for happiness, as though it lay in the things of this world, which soon pass away. Do not fall in with the customs of those who walk in the lusts of the flesh, and mind earthly things."[1]

Likewise for some of the things I've thought I wanted. They've so often proven to be only a symptom of a deeper desire; I've needed sometimes years and years to identify what was causing the itch. What I've heard when looking at a material possession was, *See that thing? You have the money. You want it. Here's your chance to have it. Now! So buy it!* But when there's only been that voice shouting at me, and no peace, I've known it was the desire of my flesh talking—and time to walk away.

When I've waited on the Lord, that's when He has delighted me by fulfilling far bigger dreams. In one instance that you'll read about later, I'd been carrying a desire around for half my life. And in that dream come true, I learned what I would have forfeited had I settled for the lesser desire that preceded it.

Hearing the Heart

A sacred pace, and especially working to get neutral, is about tuning out the noise of your mind and the world so your heart can be heard. You see, there are ears and eyes of the head, and there are ears and eyes of the heart. The entire process of getting in step with God helps you train yourself to see and hear with your heart above all.

That's not to say I don't use reason and experience to help me discern God's answers for my business and my life. As you've read, I'm very intent about due diligence. In my pursuit of the facts in any situation, I not only apply the things I've learned, but I pay attention to circumstances and seek the wisdom of trusted advisors. The Spirit uses all these things to help me drill down past any deceptive emotions, dangerous impulses, and hidden sin—all with the divine goal of getting me in touch with my true desires.

You have to give up yourself so God can have His way. As long as you are still trying to be in control, as long as you insist on your plan rather than God's, you won't get a "Spirit" answer in your decision-making; it'll be a "self" answer.

The theme of this book is to get beyond yourself and discover God's best answers for your life. If you need to talk to someone, fine. I know I sometimes need to be jarred, having somebody ask me tough questions to keep me from running off the tracks. Just don't trust your impulses; don't go with your emotions alone. When you do, you're allowing your mind too much control. And trying to solve a problem from there is sure to backfire.

Working through the steps to get neutral will help you get out of your way and want God's way. Not begrudgingly or fearfully, but gratefully. Expectantly.

This is one of the biggest changes I've experienced. I no longer live in dread, scared to death that if I don't make everything happen according to my plan, it will fail. Some of my ventures may actually fail as part of God's plan! He never promised to spare us pain, but He promised that the pain will be *purposeful*—He will use it to give us what we want most if we will do our part and let Him do His. Therefore, I try to keep moving forward in faith, doing what I can do, knowing He will then do what only He can do.

Part of my responsibility is to turn a deaf ear to the often-tempting things my flesh says will bring me satisfaction, and instead wait on the Lord for the desires of my heart. I live in complete confidence that as I operate from the heart, God will work all things for my good, my better, and my best. He said so! He will be good to me—delighting me beyond anything I could ever ask for or imagine, never making me settle for second best.

Ultimately, this process is one of giving up ourselves until we have "crucified the flesh with its passions and desires" (Gal. 5:24). This is how we die to sin and become alive to God. This is how we offer ourselves to His fulfilling purposes (Rom. 6:11–13). This is what Christ meant when He announced, "Whoever wants to be my disciple must deny themselves and take up their cross daily and follow me" (Luke 9:23).

The biblical commands to deny ourselves come with both a huge blessing and a bonus. The blessing is that we won't come to the end of our lives and discover we've gained the whole world while forfeiting our soul (Matt. 16:26). And the bonus is that God gives us the greatest desires of our heart.

Become More Whole

In the journey of discerning God's will and doing it, you have to be willing to dig deep and "know thyself," because below the surface are roots that have supported your sin for years. Idols. Walls. Emotional attachments. It's some pretty ugly stuff. Yet by now, I think you know this path involves more than removing those obstacles so you can get where you want to go. It's about doing the work to become whole so that we can look to the Lord with expectation and trust. It entails responding to the gentle nudges of the Spirit rather than the shoves of our flesh. It means letting the Master Chef take out of us or put into us any ingredient that He deems necessary.

Sometimes God has really surprised me. Where I expected discipline and pain—some salt in my wounds to teach me a lesson—He has given me something different.

Immediately after my burnout, for example, in the infancy of my faith, I expected the Lord would let me fail miserably in any new business venture. And why not? Forcing me to "marry my unfinished business," so to speak, and stay in misery for a time seemed the quickest way to make me more whole. Instead, He let me work through my pride in a positive way: by dripping success a little at a time rather than depriving me of it entirely. And discovering the process to getting neutral, where I could safely and quietly learn to let God be God and Lord over my emotions and decisions, was a significant part of that.

If I was God, I don't know that I would've been so merciful. Then again, if He had let Texon fail, I might not have changed as much. Its failure would have bruised my pride for sure, but people undergo loss all the time, only to forget its lessons once it's over. Desperation doesn't necessarily get rid of the disease that's ailing you. You have to actually put remedies into action. And God has supplied those in abundance, along with His tender care.

God's patient nurturing is what has produced long-lasting, holistic change in me. Sometimes the plant needs pruning; sometimes it needs food and water. Yet even in the pruning, we can trust that the Lord knows how much rain and how much "shine" our hearts need to grow. When we let Him tend the seed He has sowed, a harvest will come of it, for He has promised to complete His good work in us.

Fruitful Versus Productive

My ministry consultant Lynn describes the Christian life as "an external expression of an internal experience." And out of our internal experience with God comes fruitfulness. That fruitfulness is the work of the Spirit of Christ in a believer's life. Jesus said, "No branch can bear fruit by itself; it must remain in the vine. Neither can you bear fruit unless you remain in me" (John 15:4). Christians must hold high the Word of God, but if there is no friendship with Christ, no welcoming of the Spirit alongside the gospel, we can easily be pulled away from an intimate life with Him—and into an overemphasis on rules and rituals.

Becoming whole does not center on how well we perform. Lynn has taught me a very important distinction between being *fruitful* and *productive*. Fruitfulness comes from tending to what's inside; productiveness is about externals, about doing.

Without question, there's a time and place for productivity. But when it comes to matters of the heart—when it comes to tending our souls—our "work" needs to be about cultivating life in the Spirit, not marking off the little boxes on our list:

I did my devotions. *Check.*

I prayed. *Check.*

I was kind to my neighbor today. *Check.*

A life that knows and heeds God's voice, that seeks and awaits the presence of God, confident that He will make Himself known, is the life that produces a real yield, bearing much fruit.

What does a fruitful life look like? In addition to the ideas we've discussed so far, such as gaining wisdom from the Scriptures, taking times of retreat, and developing a heart that is responsive to the Spirit of God, it's important to:

- *Stay connected to what sustains you.* This involves more than choosing media that feeds you. It also means carefully tending your lifestyle. In his book *Soul Keeping,* John Ortberg talks about the difference between being busy and hurried. He says busy is when we physically have a lot to do. "Being hurried is . . . a condition of the soul. It means to be so preoccupied with myself and my life that I am unable to be fully present with God, with myself, and with other people. . . . Busy-ness migrates to hurry when we let it squeeze God out of our lives."[2]

  According to Ortberg, "busy" means having a full schedule

while "hurried" means being preoccupied. Busy can be physically demanding while hurried is spiritually draining. And being busy reminds me I need God, while being hurried causes me to be unavailable to God.

One practical way to assess how you're doing in this regard is to look at each activity on your calendar and ask: *Does this give life to my soul or deplete my soul?* If you will quiet yourself before doing this "review," most of the answers will be obvious. Then you can take the soul-depleting ones to the Lord and ask Him, through the four steps, "How should I address this?" Once you've gotten neutral, you may hear God telling you to eliminate some things, but He may also give you creative solutions for others, so that what has been a negative can become a positive, satisfying part of your life.

- *Increase your self-awareness.* Lynn says, "We just aren't suspicious enough of ourselves. We have to constantly come back from a moment and ask, 'What is within me that I felt such anger about that? What's circulating around my story that may be silently influencing my choices?'" For example, are there any negative thought patterns you need to reverse? Are you carrying around unforgiveness that is poisoning your actions or relationships? Do you know what your temperament is and what triggers you as a result? Self-understanding at all these levels helps you thrive.
- *Practice "neutral listening."* My buddy John Patchell came up with this term to describe his way of fighting through denial. "I'm not listening neutrally if I am unwilling to go to others to gather truth," he says. "Nine people out of ten in a room may know a truth about me that I don't see. What keeps me from inviting the nine to speak the obvious? What keeps me from wanting to process the truth that I hear from my mentors? Denial. Maybe I'll let the truth enter 'the sifter,' but I really

don't want to crank up the machine; if I do, the truth might sift into my soul. I'm pretty content to let it stay up there on the surface, unprocessed. Chances are, if I leave it sitting there, it will blow out of my system completely at the next wind that comes along."[3]

Do you have companions who will see and speak the truth? That close circle of friends, which hopefully includes some who have known you a long time, makes it harder to dodge reality. A reality that, if heeded, may just save you from yourself. These companions absolutely keep us on point for growth and moving toward wholeness.

• *Take inventory each year of how you've grown in the fruit of the Spirit since the previous year.* If we get complacent, we quit growing. And complacency gets us in trouble.

Finishing Well

Besides pursuing the fruitful life of the Spirit, the "whole" soul will seek to finish well.

It's vital to finish your business—the business of your life, that is—through therapy, spiritual direction, discipleship, small group and church involvement, and/or accountability partners such as mentors. Where you have unfinished business in your life, the devil has a heyday: he goes about picking off the low-hanging fruit where the flesh still rules. Where you're whole, the devil can't lure you into a bad deal; it's a waste of time for him. You have the fruit of the Spirit, and it is increasing by the day. You're reaping the harvest that is in your soul.

My therapist told me something really insightful when that public utility declined to partner with me in a new business after nine months of negotiations prior to Texon. He advised, "Terry, this was your baby, and you need to grieve. If you don't take advantage of the gift of tears that God gave you, you'll either overreact or underreact on your next major opportunity."

Being diligent about our interior work does bump us up against our sinful or wounded self, but if that's what it takes to be made more whole, then let's do it. If it will keep us at God's pace until we've finished getting neutral *and* prevent us from "misreacting" in the face of pain, then let's make that choice. It's worth all of this to be able to say with full assurance: "It is well with my soul."

Part 4

REACHING A SACRED PACE IN REAL LIFE

CHAPTER 16

WITH YOUR SPOUSE

I N THIS FINAL SECTION of the book, I want to show how aligning one's will with God plays out in some of the everyday decisions of marriage, parenting, work, stewardship, and ministry. This chapter will focus on marriage, but if you are not married, hopefully some of the principles can help you in your closest relationships. If you can quit speeding ahead and eventually get neutral at home, with the people who know you best and love you most, then you can do it in other settings and situations as well.

I have learned through the pain of my mistakes that for me to get on a sacred pace is honoring to my wife—that's where the best decisions are made. (We have less conflict that way too.) Marriage should never be a matter of, "Oh well, my spouse will get used to it." Doris and I both hang on to our positions until we have obtained peace about an answer. But in my role as a husband, it's particularly important for me to be okay with her saying no, too, not just the Lord. She is one of the gifts He's given me to help me choose and live wisely. So when I've finished gathering the facts, we both consult our Friend Jesus, note any circumstances, and see if we independently come to a peaceful joint agreement.

Until we do, we keep talking and praying.

Saving Me from Myself

If I really think the Lord knows best, then I'm less prone to stretch the truth, manipulate, or try to overpower my wife to get what I want. And to be sure, I often want *something*! In fact, I want something frequently enough that, when I present my next "proposal" to her, we are likely to share a here-we-go-again laugh before getting down to the business of seeking God's will.

Doris and I have worked hard to be compatible; agreement between us isn't automatic. In fact, our Myers-Briggs personality profiles are very opposite of each other. Regardless, one thing we've always shared is the conviction to not buy anything unless we can afford it. Neither of us came from money, and so we've never been comfortable with debt. Because I like things, however, and I'm constantly dreaming about bigger and better, we have established one overall rule about spending: we must agree to any major purchase. I do the research; Doris helps me decide. And I mean that. We don't go forward on a purchase or decision without her okay.

For one, much of the upkeep of those purchases will fall on her. I respect that and don't want to overburden her. Second, as I've said previously, many of my ideas aren't good ones anyway, so I need her grounding to keep me from doing something stupid. The Lord has used her level head many times to save me from my weaknesses.

Heeding a more sacred pace also helps us resolve conflict. There have been two times that I know of where Doris was clearly upset with me but hesitant to confront me. In those instances, aware that she was wary of my reaction, I asked the Holy Spirit to place a hedge of protection around me so I would just listen and not react. He did exactly that both times, which kept the marital lines of communication open and brought resolution.

One of those moments came up many years ago. Doris was graduating from college with a degree in psychology, but she couldn't see a way to apply her degree vocationally. While I was excited for her accomplishment, I was also preoccupied with my own thing: I was considering selling half or all of Texon. And when we were meeting with friends, I tended to focus the conversation on the Texon situation, almost to the exclusion of Doris's deliberations about her future.

Tension flared between us one night following a ministry trip, and I knew she was upset with me. Aware of how defensively I'd reacted when she'd tried to be honest about the effects of my actions in the past, I asked the Holy Spirit to surround me and subdue my reaction when we did talk about this. I figured my wife was about to point out some of my sin, which is hard to hear. Nevertheless, I wanted to remain as neutral as possible.

I'm grateful that Doris was willing to risk telling me the truth about the pride she was seeing and hearing in me regarding my business. "When you talk to other people about this possible Texon deal, Terry, you're doing more bragging than telling," she said. She also admitted to her own frustration about finding a place to use her further education.

For Doris to be able to say everything she wanted without a reaction from me helped us both. And we worked through this conflict pretty quickly.

A far bigger issue surfaced between us just a couple of years ago, when the two of us hosted an off-site marriage retreat facilitated by a couple from a national ministry. Doris and I were the oldest couple attending, and we'd been Christians longer than any of the others, so the facilitators expected us to co-lead the event. In my wife's desire to serve the process, she felt led to get involved in some of the logistics— decisions around scheduling for meals and so on. At one point the chef was unclear about the process, and Doris spoke into that. Since we weren't the hosts of the retreat facility, I felt we should stay out of it, and I said so, in front of the facilitators and guests.

"Let's just leave it to the experts," I told her.

"I'm trying to figure out how to set up the kitchen, Terry."

"Stay out of it, Doris. It's not your role," I snapped.

That one exchange between us made for a very chilly weekend.

Later, I found out that Doris had been absolutely correct in her assessment of what was needed. Nevertheless, the damage had been done. In more ways than one.

The conversation afterward was a difficult one, but also a pivotal one for our marriage, as my wife disclosed things I didn't want to admit to myself. Not only did my questioning of her in public hurt her feelings, it reopened a wound that had been there our entire relationship: Doris had never felt I completely respected her.

Wow. That cut deep. While I certainly respected her 100 percent in some areas, I couldn't say that across the board, as the Lord wanted, and she and I both knew it.

I felt such torment about how my pride had affected Doris's and my relationship that I asked Jesus to change my heart and help me respect my wife to the fullest in every area of our life together. For five months, I got on my knees every day and prayed that I would surrender myself and let God accomplish His work in me. I also found a prayer that I could pray each day for my wife, and it helped me be more mindful of her and her feelings.[1] In time, Doris saw and heard the difference in me and was able to sense my respect deep in her soul.

These days, I'm slower to confront Doris about an annoyance or hurt than I used to be. By slowing down and waiting until I am past my emotions, I can more easily evaluate whether what she's doing is really a problem to me or whether it bothers me because it's triggering a hidden issue of mine. Dealing with my own sins first makes it possible for me to speak with her about things in a less emotional, less judgmental manner. And that's important because of a question I expect to hear from the Lord when I reach heaven: "How did you treat your closest neighbor—your spouse?" If this is a question of His, my answer is a litmus test. It will reveal how much I surrendered and sacrificed for Doris. How much I have learned to love. How well I served my wife, and consequently others, rather than myself.

Kite and String

Doris and I laughingly describe our relationship as "kite and string": she allows me to fly but reels me in when I get too far out with one of my crazy ventures. Though she typically says no to my latest ideas, at least initially, this is normal in our marriage, and I'm fine with it. In fact, I know I need her to temper me. Some of my ideas are so crazy, however, that we simply have to have a heart-to-heart. This helps us slow down until clarity and neutrality prevail for both of us.

In her personal fact-gathering process, Doris needs time to ask questions and warm up to my latest idea—if one of those out-of-the-box ideas is even worth considering.

If we're looking at a sizable purchase, for example, she doesn't want to consider it unless I'm really serious about it. She has often had me rank my interest level from one to ten. If it is over a five, our agreement is that I must make sure the Lord has given me the okay to proceed to the next step before I bring her in. It's also important that I allow time for Him to show *her* His desire, not just me.

Prime example: I almost bought a large boat two months after the sale of one of our divisions. A boat owner had told me, "It's so much better to see the land from the ocean than to see the ocean from the land." And with that in mind, I was thinking this beautiful vessel that I had my eye on was a desire of my heart. To Doris, it was a clear *no* from start to finish. She'd never been fond of the seafaring life—so there was no way she wanted to own a boat. Besides, she was aware I was in a season where my pride was at its height, which is never the time for me to be making major purchases.

I finally hit the brakes and took this decision to the Lord—and when I wasn't able to get any peace about it, I backed out of the deal.

There's nothing wrong with owning a boat or anything else if you can afford it, but only if blessed and approved by the Lord.

I'm very thankful now that Doris stood her ground. Her conviction pushed me to work to get neutral about this purchase and let God decide what was best for both of us. This situation did, though, awaken a desire in me to have a breathtaking view of the land from the water. I wasn't sure what the Lord might do with that desire, but to this day, I've been at peace with not owning a boat.

The Coast

There is one purchase decision in particular that still makes me marvel at how the Lord works. It is also close to my heart because of how God brought my wife and me into agreement as we both sought Him over many, many years.

It all began back in about 1983, when Doris and I started vacationing on the central California coast. In our first visits there, we stayed at a hotel with views of Big Sur. We enjoyed sitting on our balcony at sunset, dreaming and talking while we took in the beauty of the ocean.

During one of those first balcony conversations, I noticed a particular house in the distance, situated on a bluff above the ocean, and I remarked, "Who would be lucky enough to live there? I'd sure like to be able to buy that place someday." This was prior to my burnout, and the lustful dreamer in me was operating at full throttle, as he always did in those days, and so Doris just let my comment slide.

Eventually the two of us returned, and then we kept returning, because we fell in love with that area. Especially as a getaway location. It was very peaceful to both of us. Secluded, beautiful—a spot where we could truly escape the stresses of life.

Intent on finding a permanent place there, I started touring properties more earnestly in 2010. I did it so much that Doris finally protested,

"Whenever we go to California, the house hunt is taking away from *us*." So I said, "Okay, I won't make you look at any more real estate." We rented a place instead and focused on spending time together.

The realtor did, however, continue to send me information as houses in that area came on the market. Not surprisingly, the ones that appealed to me most were always overlooking the water. But through 2010 and 2011, I didn't have peace about buying anything permanent, in spite of having sold two Texon divisions in that time.

Come January 2012, the realtor sent me an email saying the house on the bluff was on the market. When I saw the flyer, I instantly knew that was the location we'd seen in the distance nearly thirty years earlier—and I wanted it. But Doris didn't want any more properties, and I knew I wasn't yet neutral since it was only about five months after the latest business sale. I put it out there anyway, showing her the pictures and details a few times. She wasn't interested.

We went to the coast again in late May. The day before we left, I asked, "Would you be willing to look at just this one place? If not, our marriage is more important than a piece of real estate."

She reluctantly conceded. "I didn't want to feel any guilt at keeping Terry from this dream," she says in retrospect, "so I figured I'd have a look to honor him. But I also reminded him, 'Terry, you always have a dream.'"

When we walked in, Doris immediately liked the home because it was smaller. A big view but a smaller house. It felt simple to her.

Abiding by our rule that we don't decide on a property while we're standing on its grounds, we told the realtor we'd think about it, and we went home to pray and consider what God would have us do. I remained willing for Doris and the Lord to say no, but I certainly had a preference: I hoped the answer would be a yes!

Not long after we returned from that trip, somebody made an offer on the house next door, and we mistakenly thought it was the one we'd toured. At that point Doris said, "You know, if you want it, make an offer." That instance of mistaken identity broke Doris loose and put her at peace about owning the home if it all worked out. She was gaining a vision for it as a place of retreat for individuals who needed a new setting in which to be restored and renewed. So we made an offer.

We closed on it in August 2012—one full year after my latest liquidity event—and got the house at a price well below listing. And here's the sweetness of the Lord in all of this to me: the first time I went to the house by myself for a retreat, I realized, *I got my boat.* Not because the house feels big, but because of its location.

The place was built to pay tribute to God's creation as soon as you walk in, and that's what really matters. It literally sits on a point *in* the Pacific. The pelicans and seagulls fly by only feet away; you're surrounded by waves and water to the left and the right and below you; the ocean breezes blow constantly across the width of the house as it would on a boat; and from the various windows inside, I can view the hotels and houses dotting the shoreline—just as I could if I was watching from a bow. What's more, this "land vessel" won't depreciate or require as much upkeep as a boat, which brings joy to Doris's heart too.

To realize how unexpectedly God fulfilled this long-held desire of my heart was a profoundly personal and spiritual moment for me. I felt the Lord's love so deep in my soul, and I will never forget it. I couldn't have manufactured all the circumstances to make it happen—especially having my wife's blessing after nearly thirty years of wondering and waiting. And in retrospect, I'm glad I didn't try. This was such a powerful lesson! The moment of decision was that much sweeter because Doris and I were in agreement with the Lord, the three of us moving forward together at His pace rather than mine.

I firmly believe: God's loving-kindnesses are on display in our lives each day. My marriage to someone who will stand firm until we get neutral together is my constant reminder of this.

CHAPTER 17
....

WHEN PARENTING

O UR GIRLS, TANYA AND Jeannie, were in seventh and
fourth grades when I burned out, so Doris and I didn't start
getting neutral in our parenting until after that. Yet we saw the positive impact of this approach, and the girls speak of it as well. In fact,
now that they are parents themselves, they are raising their kids with
an eye to the Lord's will on the tough decisions, such as when to
homeschool.

As Tanya says, "The Lord's answers haven't always been easy, but
we've still been able to walk them out. Things have come to light in
the process of obeying God's answers that wouldn't have otherwise."

A Plus for Parents

Plenty of times, taking the time to align ourselves with the Lord's
desires helps us moms and dads as much or more than it benefits our
kids. My friend Gary has a daughter who was thinking of marrying a
young man who was between jobs. Gary hired the boyfriend (Dean)
to work for his construction company. Pretty quickly, Gary got wind
that Dean was compromising certain company policies. Gary prayed
about this situation each day, watched for circumstances, and was
especially careful to gather as many facts as possible. He spoke to

people who had seen firsthand what Dean was doing. Gary consulted Human Resources. He also sought the advice of a mentor who asked him a lot of questions to help him think through his response. After Gary got neutral, he waited for God's answer. And as soon as he had it, he called his daughter and told her, "I'm letting Dean go."

Her response was immediate. "I can't believe this! I don't know who's going to walk me down the aisle, but it won't be you!"

On the phone with his mentor right after this conversation, Gary could still affirm, "I have all the peace in the world that I need to let Dean go."

Even Gary's wife didn't want him firing Dean. Nonetheless, he'd obtained clarity from the Lord, and he had 100 percent certainty that this was the answer.

In the midst of this decision, God had shown Gary a bigger issue in his own heart than whether to fire Dean: Gary came face-to-face with the fact that he had idolized his daughter and treated her as his queen—rather than saving that distinction for his wife. This had bred dysfunction both in their family dynamics and in his daughter's dating relationship. So, to risk not walking her down the aisle was very significant. Still, he recognized the Lord's answer when it came, and he knew he had to follow where the peace was, letting God take care of the rest.

"I'd always gone along with the ways of the world," he says. "I'd always cared what other people thought. Especially my daughter. But this time, I had so much peace, even her verbal jabs didn't sway me."

Here's the rest of the story: Gary and his wife continued to pray for the Lord's will in their daughter's life and in their household. One day, their daughter went to a therapy session and came home crying. She and Dean had been moving fast toward buying a house and a ring, but in that session she realized, "This is not the right guy for me." Years later, she married someone else, and Gary did walk her down the aisle.

For Doris and me, choosing a sacred pace has helped us in the midst of those inevitable moments of decision with kids. We were able to be less reactive and more proactive in our parenting. I have to credit my therapist for a particular observation about raising teenagers that kept me on course with my girls as they got older. He said, "Teens rebel to get the courage to leave home." Once he told me that, I was better able to do what I needed to do as a dad, and also to be able to support Doris as she navigated things mother-to-daughter.

For example, one of the girls had multiple fender benders in high school. Whenever this daughter would call home about another accident or come home with a dented car, Doris would naturally get upset and want to react. But I'd say, "Okay, if the neighbor's daughter had a wreck just like that, how would you rank its seriousness from 1 to 10?" Then I'd ask, "What would you recommend *that* mother do?" This allowed her to more quickly get neutral and make sure the punishment fit the crime.

Our Kids Too

Slowing down to get neutral helps our kids too.

It's been very touching to see our daughters take up this practice and let the Lord work in their own lives and hearts. I particularly saw its impact when Jeannie and her fiancé, Trey, were making wedding plans.

Back in middle school, Jeannie preceded Pinterest by creating a wedding portfolio in a three-ring binder to showcase the ideas she liked best. She added to it regularly over the years, and by the time she was actually engaged, her binder contained more possibilities than could ever be accomplished in one event. When the time came for us to sit down and go over her plans, I was concerned. Having consistently heard her mention the elaborate things she had in mind, I knew the biggest weekend of her life was going to be her biggest disappointment if something didn't change, because her mother and I had set a budget commensurate with her sister's wedding.

Jeannie understood that our numbers would not remotely cover everything she'd been planning. But rather than begging us to increase the budget, as some daughters would, she and Trey submitted their desires about their wedding to the Lord. Their conclusion? Having learned that God uses tithing as an internal "reset" to enable us to contentedly live within our means, the bride- and groom-to-be felt led by the Lord to step out in faith and tithe 10 percent of their wedding budget.

As Jeannie sought and obeyed the Lord's answer, He changed her heart. In return, she received the desire of her heart: their tithe made a difference for others *and* she enjoyed a dream wedding day without bending the budget.

In this instance, God used tithing as the means to my daughter's joy, but He could choose a different means for someone else. The important thing is that the process of reaching neutral gave Jeannie and Trey a fresh perspective, and God quietly showed them creative ways to make the budget work. With their new mindset, it was more than enough. And Jeannie's joy was multiplied because her wedding day wasn't tainted with thoughts of *I wish we'd done something else instead.*

Jeannie reflects now: "My parents always exemplified the idea of 'Hold on loosely.' We grew up tithing. We grew up in a generous home and were taught that no matter how small your checking account, live out of a generous heart and mind. My personality is to make the best of whatever I'm given. So the best thing Trey and I could think of was to honor the Lord and tithe from our wedding budget. We just knew it was the right thing to do."

Doris and I were so proud that the two of them chose to get in step with God as a couple over one of the first major decisions of their lives together. If they were able to do this on such an important occasion, we knew they'd take other issues to the Lord once they were married.

A Sacred Pace When They're Older

Even with our daughters grown, married, and raising kids of their own, Doris and I still have to opt for God's will and wait on the Lord. Understandably, we parents often feel the urge to guide (or sometimes push!) our grown children in a particular direction because, well, *they're still our kids*! But this is something we must resist, and the steps help.

A few years back, when our oldest daughter, Tanya, and her husband were presented with an opportunity to take a new job overseas, we longed for them to remain stateside. At that time, they had a three-year-old, a one-year-old, and a baby on the way. However, as Doris and I began to slow down and submit to the Lord's direction, and as our loved ones also prayerfully processed their options, we were convinced to let God direct Tanya and Brannin's steps. (They ended up moving out of state but remaining in the States.) Tanya has since expressed that neither she nor Brannin felt pressured to stay close to home. In fact, they felt released and encouraged to go anywhere the Lord was calling them. This was reassuring for both Doris and me to hear, because it was important to us to not interfere with God's work in our family's life.

To willingly wait and learn the Lord's desires not only blesses us with deep peace as parents but also becomes a great gift to our children and their families. We must be willing, though, to hold our tongues until, if, and when God opens the door for us to do so.

My therapist has advised, "Don't give advice or correct blind spots in your adult children unless they ask." No grown man or woman likes unsolicited suggestions, whether he or she is related to us or not. An unsolicited offering of truth to any adult is dangerous business—often worse than not speaking up at all. You become the villain unless they've sought you out. And people will avoid a villain at all costs, which means losing the opportunity to speak into the situation altogether.

171

So what do you do in those instances where you see your grown child heading down a disappointing path? One mom, Tina, decided to "shut up and pray." In slowing down and working to get neutral, she realized that being right wasn't as important to her as maintaining a relationship with her adult son, Colin. Rather than making the mistake of giving him an ultimatum (which experts say should be reserved for situations where a person is endangering themselves or others), she waited for the Lord to open the conversational doors. Once Colin came to her and her husband for guidance, Tina was in a mindset where she could speak the truth softly, have it be heard, and still leave the decision to him.

Colin has persisted in some choices that she doesn't agree with, and he is facing some less-than-ideal consequences as a result. And though Tina wishes he would do the right thing, God has given her peace on three levels. First, the lines of communication between mother and son are still open, which was the real desire of her heart all along. Second, she was able to lovingly speak the truth and have it be heard. And third, she's able to support Colin in the many positive decisions he *is* making because she didn't let this one decision drive a wedge between them.

To parent in partnership with the Lord doesn't mean you just casually let your kids have their way. It does mean you submit your plans (and theirs) to God and let Him show you a way through as a family. You may end up responding in ways that sometimes surprise them—and that might surprise you as parents. But that's okay. Our God is a God of surprises. He's also the best Parent of all, so He can be trusted.

As mothers and fathers, we should always be practicing a sacred pace with our children. By doing so, we will leave a legacy of faith in the Lord that survives us for generations to come.

CHAPTER 18
·····························

WHILE AT WORK

Texon is not a heavy-asset company. This means that our business doesn't rely on manufacturing—people are the most critical assets we have. Thus, we are particularly careful about personnel decisions. And while not every employee or executive at Texon is a person of faith, nor are they required to be, I've tried to encourage a workplace environment that quietly honors God in its ways of doing business. Among other things, this means ensuring that we go the extra mile with whomever we hire and striving hard to honor anyone we ever have to let go.

In the spring of 2016 we laid off employees for the first time in company history. It took me and my leadership team many, many months to finalize this decision—with me personally seeking God's guidance at every step. I agonized over it for close to a year as I watched oil prices bottom out. Though we couldn't find a way to spare the jobs of these faithful employees, the Lord revealed ways that we could honor them. And one of those ways was to give them unexpected bonuses in addition to robust severances. These people had done so much to contribute to our past success, and we wanted them to know their efforts were recognized. It was also important to me to have some time with each of them individually before they left, in order to tell them how much I'd appreciated working with them. Though I might be facing some very angry people, our core values of service and relationships apply internally, not just with customers. I wasn't willing to make this an impersonal, let-HR-handle-it situation.

On their last day in the office, I sat down with these men and women one by one for a heart-to-heart. I planned to affirm them very specifically and wanted to know how they were doing—but I also intended to give them a place to say whatever was on their minds. Going into that Friday, my spirit was so heavy; I expected it to be one of my worst days ever. But to a person, they were so gracious! In fact, their responses were a true encouragement to me. Over and over, they thanked me for providing a positive place to work and expressed appreciation for our generosity. One of the best things was hearing that their severances were enough to fund career changes that they were excited about. One individual was looking forward to becoming a wedding planner; another, a realtor, and so on. It made me feel like the Lord honored our desire to honor our people, even though this process was painful for everyone. It also confirmed the importance of hiring good people and doing right by them every chance you get.

Resolving Conflict

Spend enough time with anyone—coworkers, family, friends—and you'll inevitably have conflict. That's just the nature of relationships. What do you do then?

At Texon, we've learned the hard way that to delay confrontation lets a negative situation continue. Yet it's all about timing, because to speak or react out of frustration with someone in the workplace is speaking out of the wrong place—and it's never received well. So, we must have the hard conversations, but in the proper spirit (ideally, by the Spirit). Upholding the value of truthful, authentic communication not only honors the people we work with but layers our conversations in integrity.

One way to honor anyone in these emotionally charged situations is to talk with them face-to-face rather than confronting via email. (This is true with customers as well, not just coworkers.) Not everybody works in-house anymore, but employees who work remotely can still be FaceTimed or Skyped if something needs to be discussed. And if they can't be contacted this way, then a phone call is your next best option, because it's still immediate, live, and allows for tone to be heard, not just words. (One way I can tell if I'm trying to maintain a healthy relationship with somebody is whether I'm willing to talk with them live. Certainly, there are times when written communication is called for, but we can really damage our relationships by choosing email. If I'm dodging behind an email to avoid someone or something—either out of fear or laziness—I will pay a price.)

Undoubtedly, every company faces personnel issues. Not every workplace conflict is a one-to-one, peer-to-peer problem. What do we do to handle these situations corporately? Here's how Ronnie Andrews, our COO and a man of strong faith, gets in step with God before addressing personnel issues:

1. Pray for the Holy Spirit to reveal any judgment, hidden fears, or areas in my life that are causing or contributing to the conflict, or other sin in my life that needs to be dealt with before I talk to the person.
2. Pray for the other person's deepest needs, asking the Holy Spirit to reveal to me what that individual holds as most important.
3. Recognize that I seldom have all the facts and that things are seldom what they seem.
4. Empathize with the person's needs and feelings.
5. Repeat steps 1 through 4 until frustration, judgment, and fear are gone and I have gotten neutral in each of these areas.

6. Speak to the person about the topic in the ways in which God has guided me.
7. Listen well to both what is being said and what is going unsaid.
8. Seek to honor him or her as we talk and work toward a resolution.

Work-Life Balance

Obviously, resolving conflict isn't the only workplace challenge; finding a balance between one's job and one's life beyond the job is challenging too. It's an important consideration for each of us individually, but if we are bosses, we have an even greater responsibility to be mindful of this balance on behalf of our employees.

From the inception of Texon, I didn't want a double standard. If a forty-hour workweek was my cap, then no one I hired would be expected to work beyond that either. Trying to function according to a sacred pace ever since then has had a profound effect in my work and in the establishing of our corporate culture. Now I'm much quicker to ask: *Who's running who? Is Texon running me, or am I running Texon?*

Anyone can ask this of their job, whether you're a boss or not. If your work (even if you're self-employed) leaves nothing for family, friends, church, or anything else, then you need to take it to the Lord. Each one of us, regardless of our employer or position, has to stand against any situation where we're not allowed any quality of life. That rebellion can take many positive forms—speaking up and trying to effect change, setting personal boundaries, opting for a better work environment, and so forth.

The point is to take steps to preserve margin for ourselves on all fronts—emotionally, spiritually, mentally, physically—so that we can thrive.

Balanced, Not Burned Out

What advice can I offer you around this topic? Actually, quite a bit, thanks to being forced to learn better life choices following my burnout. Though, if you're not open to the pain that comes with change, little of what I am about to say will be of value to you. You see, my best emotional growth and maturity seems only to happen while I'm in a season of pain or have just come out of one. So don't be shocked if you have to endure some difficulty. The upside is fewer negative consequences.

Here are several additional ideas that can help you achieve a better balance and the more abundant life Jesus spoke of:

1. *Learn to say no.* No is a discipline and a protection. Most of us tend to want to help people, but as I've admitted, I'm pridefully motivated sometimes to say yes just as much because of the prestige or instant gratification a yes might bring. I constantly remind myself: I've much more often said yes and wish I'd said no; I've almost never wished that my no had been yes.

2. *Follow the peace.* This is a good rule of thumb for a team of believers who are trying to move in one accord. Within my executive team at Texon, we are in the habit of being patient and waiting on the Lord for His answer in our various areas of responsibility. When someone has gotten neutral and feels that ensuing sense of peace, they'll typically report that in our team meetings and then, as best they can, convey how they arrived at it. Unusual as it is, we try to follow that peace wherever it takes us corporately.

3. *Instill accountability into your life so you stay on track.* Therapy has been huge for me in this regard, as well as regular mentoring and weekly one-on-one discipleship.

4. *Cultivate empowering habits to keep you strong and growing.* Exercise, careful eating, daily devotional and Scripture reading, prayer, books that feed my soul—these are all parts of my regular "strength-training" routine. I've also found there is real value in writing down my thanks during Thanksgiving weekend and listing answered prayers at year's end. (Or you could turn these into weekly or monthly times of reflection if that works better for you.) Gratitude and remembrance are two of the greatest disciplines because they stimulate a God-honoring mindset all year round. You'll never be sorry you added them to your life.

5. *Eliminate any double standards.* Our motto at Texon is "Do the right thing." I tell employees that this includes challenging me on an issue if I need to be challenged. Whether it's the workplace or your marriage, a church meeting or a family squabble, there's no balance in a situation where only one person or group of people has a say. By actively seeking the input of others, you can make sure you're not creating or supporting that kind of environment.

6. *Take your allotted vacation time from work.* Goodness, we all need some time away from the routine to be refreshed and restored! You will be a better person—and better in all your roles (employee/boss, spouse, parent, etc.) upon your return.

7. *If you're married, go away alone with your spouse at least once a year.* Ideally, I recommend doing this at least three times a year. You both need a break from your day-to-day. This will do wonders for your life together, especially helping you both to remember why you got married in the first place.

8. *Get away by yourself for two days every six months for some real solitude and a self-review.* Trust me, this is life-changing. No newspaper or TV. Try not to answer too many emails. Don't take work with you. Truly get quiet so you can reflect and

spend some time with the Lord, doing any internal business that's needed.

Some people go away more frequently than this, and some people plan a simple agenda for their time away. But most of us don't "retreat" at all. Getting out of the house and out of your routine does wonders for maintaining balance. Sometimes I focus on re-experiencing and being overwhelmed by Jesus' love for me; sometimes I do things that restore my soul, and in those simple pleasures, He comes to me very personally.

Here's an equation from Mark Batterson that helps it all make sense to me: *Change of pace + Change of place = Change of perspective.* When you turn off the world and slow down to see what the Holy Spirit may want to impart, the outcome is incredible. While I was on one of these outings a few years ago, the price of oil dropped significantly, and we as a leadership team were all tempted to react too quickly out of fear. By the time I got back in the office, though, I was in a mindset where I could wait until the Lord revealed what to do. These days away help me to listen better.

9. *Live as if your time (and every other resource) is finite—because it is.* One of the blessings of finite hours in a week is that it can give you amazing discernment about how to spend your time. God will set the boundaries if you'll ask Him to. On forty hours a week with Texon, I could still be relational with my family and fulfill God's clear calling to start a company. But God was in control of all my hours—and with the way I'd been living, He needed to be.

I'm not the only one who has discovered the wisdom in this. I attended a meeting recently of a small group of entrepreneurs. Our facilitator was the founder and CEO of Hobby Lobby, David Green, whom *Forbes* magazine labeled "the Biblical Billionaire." He goes home at five o'clock every day—and has for decades. Though he does work on Saturdays until three, he does not own a smartphone or a tablet. He also gives away so much of his income that he has become "the largest evangelical benefactor in the world."[1] And yet: his stores are closed on Sundays and the company has no long-term debt. He is someone who seeks "great" rather than just "good." Without a work-life balance, you will most likely keep doing what's "good" and miss out on the "great" that God is calling you to.

10. *Develop a mission statement for your life.* It took me five years to finalize mine[2], but my mission of "Liberating souls to help people grow to emotional and spiritual maturity through discipleship, mentoring, and support of such ministries" has become both a beacon for everything I do and a useful boundary in deciding where to invest my energies and resources. For instance, I had always wanted to be on the pastoral search committee at church. When the time came not that long ago, I talked to my mentor about it, anticipating that I might be asked to serve. To my surprise, he said it didn't sound as if it fit my mission. After getting neutral about it, I agreed that I wouldn't serve if asked. It turns out the meetings were every Sunday night for months, and additional hours were needed for reviewing résumés and listening to each candidate's "sample" sermons. Considering the number of hours it involved, this was one of many times when knowing my purpose was a huge blessing. With your mission statement as your guidepost, you can be more fully engaged in what God wants you doing on this earth—and let others pursue what He intends for them.

11. *Value your values.* They are another compass point. Figure out what's important to you, your business, and your family; write

down those guiding principles; discuss them with your loved ones and your team to constantly reinforce them—and then live by them!

....

A Note to Leaders

I'm convinced that, as a leader, if I'm drawing on the Lord to make good choices with how I manage my time, my heart, and my mind, He will help me manage my team.

From the very beginning of Texon, it was important to me to staff the company sufficiently so our employees were not overworked. Especially after my own experience of burnout, I view the overworking of employees as bad economics. Whenever you drive your own or anyone else's best gifts into overtime—past the optimum level the Lord intended—you haven't enhanced results; you've only multiplied intensity, stress, and effort. Too much overtime can ruin productivity. Period. Once you push people beyond capacity, it damages them and diminishes returns.

For me personally, restricting my workweek forced me to rely more on the Lord and be more discerning with my time. I had to learn to allocate what time I did have in the best way possible, being more selective about which customers and ventures to pursue and which ones to pass by. And I started to view my work differently: maybe I could only accomplish two or three major tasks in a day. Maybe I wasn't supposed to do those other things in the first place. Maybe they should be delegated to people who would own them and find joy in them.

When you get delusional about your ability to take on extra things, you set no limits. And eventually this wears you out. To restrict your work hours takes faith and much discipline. But I have been able to have a life—and so can my employees.

Here are a few other boundaries God helped me set for myself once I asked Him how He wanted me to conduct business:

1. *Delegate.* I am constantly delegating the things that someone else can do (usually better than me) and moving things off my plate.
2. *Assign ownership.* It's important to make sure that one person in your organization owns any given project, and that it's not you, the leader. But you also have to make sure that whoever owns it has sufficient time so that he or she may be able to do his or her *existing* work well.
3. *Drop strategically.* If your project list is already long and you take on another commitment, something's going to give— either by default (which usually means relationships suffer), or you can be proactive and decide what you'll discontinue. If you remember, this is what I did in my twenties when my health was starting to suffer from handling too many product lines. That strategic "drop" made an immediate difference in my health. Often, the results of such decisions, when done right, can be seen almost instantly.
4. *Remember who's really in charge.* Viewing success or failure as "my responsibility" causes undue pressure. Install God as your CEO, and see how this changes your perspective.

A Work in Progress

I'm busy, often too busy. And while I'm not the best at time management, these things have helped me see the benefit of a better work-life balance.

The level of joy I have is a major benefit of seeking a balance that follows a sacred pace. I am a sinner, yet I'm so much happier and fulfilled because I'm assured that most of the things I'm doing are for the right reason. Additionally, my track record shows that I make better business decisions when I live by these markers.

I don't always get it right. Sometimes I veer off course and get too busy again. But trying to stay in step with God, even in my work life, makes me quicker to course correct. What's more, if I'm focused on pleasing God, I'm less inclined to do what I shouldn't be doing and more able to follow the Lord's leading so that I do right by my colleagues as well.

CHAPTER 19

DURING NEGOTIATIONS

To THIS DAY, THERE'S almost nothing I enjoy more than working a deal. It's just that now—after my burnout and learning the necessity of operating at a slower pace—I no longer force the deal just to get one done.

I've been trained to hold deal points and plans loosely as I seek the Lord. It's definitely a discipline—a lifestyle, even—but I embrace it. For one, holding loosely makes it far tougher for people to hook you emotionally or financially. The right path also seems to stand out more clearly whenever God does choose to reveal it.

I feel it's necessary to remain wide open to the Lord since I never know initially which deals are within His will and which ones aren't. On the front end, so many of them look like they'll make Texon a lot of money. Nonetheless, I've seen the price of commodities drop significantly about five times during my career, so how can I predict what opportunity might be good for the company? A facility might get hit by lightning, or a key client might be bought out, or any number of unforeseen things could happen. Without holding things loosely, I won't receive information with the weight it deserves: I'll either discount it or try and bend it to fit what I want.

It's so important to practice slowing down and getting neutral if at all possible. Especially when selling and acquiring businesses. We once bought a propane terminal from a major oil company and had a sophisticated commercial team running data, making projections, and doing analysis. Even with the combined expertise and experience within our group (more than one hundred years of experience in the industry), we were wrong in several of our assumptions. It took a lot longer to reach market share than we anticipated. And not one of us predicted that, of all things, the increased demand of an unusually cold winter is what would make that terminal finally profitable.

Though I wanted very badly to sell our butane business back in 2010, I held the very protracted process—and consequently, the negotiations—lightly in my heart and soul, since I wasn't certain of God's desired outcome. After the sale, the buyer's key negotiator expressed his biggest concern: that I might keep the business. I took that as a sign from God that I was at peace with whatever direction the negotiations might take.

For me to negotiate big deals using my four-step process confounds people; they don't know what to do with it. On the one hand, they perceive me to be in a power position because I don't act or appear overanxious. But power is not my intent. I really want to strive to do the right thing for both parties. And I definitely can think more clearly when I am at peace regardless of the outcome.

Getting neutral and remaining there for the duration of a negotiation is also very helpful because it helps you tune in to the subtleties you might otherwise miss. For example, I have discovered that if I listen without an agenda, the other party will start coaching me about what they want. And that simplifies the entire deal. It also lets me stay calm and objective and not close too soon, even if I am clear on the other person's priorities. For the sake of integrity, I also don't shake hands on an agreement until I'm certain about going forward. The length of time it takes for me to get there can vary, but I usually need at least twenty-four hours, away from the intensity of a meeting, to spend time with the Lord and make sure my excitement hasn't misled me.

If you're careful not to prematurely suggest you have a deal, you can walk away should the Holy Spirit say, "Forget it," or if He reveals a piece of the negotiation you're not comfortable with.

The Ground Rules

I truly believe that how we operate as a company in this particular area of sales and negotiations has been critical to our success. It is also an area in which we've been practicing a slower pace for a very long time. I'm convinced this is no coincidence.

Here are my ground rules for business negotiations. These are guidelines God has guided me to, and they have proven to be huge blessings to me and to Texon.

- *Always understand the downside risk.* My worst-case assumption is that oil could fall to half its current value and another major recession will happen within two years. I think through potential deals with the downside as my baseline so that I don't overoptimistically consider something that might potentially hurt us badly.
- *Don't chase targets, and beware of metrics.* When commissions, quotas, or sales goals are what's driving you, *you* become the priority, not the customer. When that happens, you won't see the kind of success you would if you were focused on customer service. We have no metric goals at Texon—our goal is to develop long-term relationships with our customers. Yet for several years, before selling our two largest divisions, we were among the top five private revenue-earning companies in Houston. Repeat business is a byproduct of relationships. You don't have to sell if trust and goodwill have been established.

- *Hold off on an offer until you know what the other person wants.* (We also do this in hiring key employees.) In other words, listen until you can help your customer accomplish his or her goals. Yes, it takes patience to let that prospective customer or employee coach you about what to propose, but if you pay attention and refuse to rush the front end, your offer will be very honoring, and you can structure a much better outcome, saving everyone time and money.

  Incidentally, not doing a deal should be a win/win too. By that, I mean if either of you opt not to sign on the dotted line, it should be because that's best for both of you. Also, if you tick people off, you lose. Every time. But if you'll keep the dialogue open and work hard at resolving problems, then even if you don't land a deal this time, you've built trust and you anchor with the customer in a way that will make them more likely to approach you another time.

- *Redefine your sales role.* You must get in your soul that it's not your role to actually convince someone; your role as a salesperson is to listen, to help, to support, and to serve customers. When you start selling, you quit listening. And when you quit listening, you limit the impact that the facts, the customer, or the Lord would have had in the decision-making process. Anytime you don't get the full picture of your customer's wants (because you think you already know), it will cost you. Not just in a worse final price but in longer negotiations, unnecessary delays, and less relational trust. You miss out on so much if you get too focused on the sale. Seeking to serve rather than to sell changes the dynamics entirely—and for the better.

- *Focus on needs versus price.* Sometimes prospective customers will ask, "What's the price?" But we don't do things that way. We always teach new salespeople to find out the customer's real needs, continue to seek more information, and focus on serving them well so that the customer is happy. Hearing a client so carefully that you can tailor a deal to his or her priorities usually means that both parties have a better deal.

- *Deal one-on-one when possible.* My motto is, "One-on-one over a meal" when sensitive or transparent conversations need to be had. The more people you add to the talks, the less the intimacy. And less intimacy usually means less relational connection, and thus, less information and progress.

While I was in negotiations to sell the crude-oil business, my contact at the potential buyer was so "done" with the discussions that he wanted to quit the deal altogether. So I asked him to dinner. He was expecting a tug-of-war, but I wasn't selling that night. I had spent time getting neutral prior to the meeting and was even more aware of intentionally listening to God as we met. So I just decided to let the conversation unfold and follow this guy's lead about what we discussed. It surprised him that I wasn't pushing him to work with us. And by the end of the evening, he announced, "I'm not quitting!"

No matter the size of the deal, you simply can't replace the benefits of having prepared your heart in God's presence before meeting with someone. Ideally, you want to remain neutral throughout every conversation from start to finish. If you get emotional, it will cost you. If people try to muscle you, being neutral will keep you from getting caught up in that.

- *Leave something on the table.* I try to leave money on the table to create a mutual win-win. This also develops long-term relationships and encourages repeat business.
- *When you have to say no, never defend your answer with numbers.* My process is to reveal my heartfelt conviction rather than any financial facts behind my decision. Facts and numbers can be argued with; feelings are much harder for people to discount.

Unconventional

I'm very aware of how unconventional all of this is. Just remember, I am a lifelong deal junkie and a salesman at heart. So I live these principles; I'm not just suggesting them from some remote corner office.

What's more, other companies besides mine see the value of a slower pace. One business leader I know told me that he and his team have worked to slow down and seek the Lord's will in numerous corporate deals, including some pretty high-risk scenarios.

Here's an instance he has shared with me:

We had a longtime business supplier that was acquired by a bigger company, but the buyer didn't want to do business with us. Two law firms said they'd take up our case on contingency and felt confident about our success if we sued. So I went to our leadership team, and seven of the eight said, "Yes, let's sue!" But I couldn't get peace around it.

Upon getting neutral, I knew that I wasn't supposed to sue. I had 100 percent peace about this. So I went back and told our team, "Not only could I not get peace about suing, I in fact have peace around *not* suing, even though I think it's going to hurt us financially and corporately."

This really set us back on our heels. It didn't feel team-honoring to me, but it did feel God-honoring. And that's what I had to trust. Amazingly, over time, those team members came to me one by one and quietly admitted, "I think you're doing the right thing." And later, God sprinkled us with some business from out of nowhere.

Usually I have a view of what's coming, but this time I didn't. I sat in my prayer closet and wept because I felt like God honored my willingness to take the risk and listen to Him.

There's certainly great personal benefit to processing through the four steps in all major decisions. But to do so in your day-to-day operations and seek to honor others above your bottom line? Well, the payoffs are huge there too! Your customers will see the difference, your employees will feel it, and God will honor it. You can't lose by doing business God's way.

CHAPTER 20

IN MINISTRY AND GIVING

WHAT DO YOU THINK is the greatest gift God has given me since my burnout? Besides the sheer goodness of His grace, I can't help but be thankful for the way He has used the process of getting neutral to greatly reduce the grip of greed as I make decisions in my life. Since embracing what God advises regarding financial stewardship, I am less of a slave to money or what it can buy.

That freedom has actually made me *more* money with less anxiety. The Bible says that if you want wealth too much, it will ruin you (1 Tim. 6:10). I have found that functioning according to God's pace has allowed me to make better business deals. And giving to ministries voluntarily, with joy and not out of obligation, has shown me how to make a greater impact with those dollars.

I am in awe that Jesus could change my heart in so many areas, but especially in this one. It is a real joy to see lives changed. Donating to ministries is like investing in business, except with exponentially greater returns. Giving to organizations and institutions that help people liberate their souls or know Christ as their Lord and Savior fulfills me till I'm flowing over.

I love how God operates toward us when we give. He promises in

Malachi 3:10 that when His people present their tithes and offerings for His use rather than withholding them for their own purposes, He throws open the very floodgates of heaven and pours out an overflowing measure of blessing. Proverbs 11:25 says, "A generous person will prosper; whoever refreshes others will be refreshed." In Deuteronomy 15:10, the Lord commanded His people to give generously to the needy among them, "and do so without a grudging heart; then because of this the LORD your God will bless you in all your work and in everything you put your hand to."

The prospering and blessing that Scripture speaks of isn't always about material wealth; there are many other types of riches, such as the righteousness, mercy, comfort, perseverance, and peace mentioned in the Beatitudes in Matthew 5. But the sum of God's promises to us is that when we are generous toward others, whether we have little or much to offer, He multiplies His generosity toward us—and we always reap the dividends.

Dually Neutral

Knowing firsthand how materialism can enslave a person, I've found it's essential to stay on a slower, prayerful pace long enough to get neutral about your decisions to give, not just about what you decide to buy.

One summer, when I took two days of time away from the hustle to be with the Lord, He guided me to start redirecting my resources to discipleship efforts. My stewardship consultant had been telling me for years, "You need to narrow your giving," but until God narrowed the parameters, I wasn't clear on what to change. In that time of careful waiting and listening on an issue that was so close to my heart, the Lord awakened me to how passionate I was about discipleship— investing in others to help them become authentic followers of Christ whose intimacy with Jesus influences every part of who they are and how they live. God then provided strategic donation opportunities for better fulfilling that passion, that desire of my heart.

Doris and I used to have disagreements about our giving—not because she didn't want us to be generous, but because she didn't feel it was good stewardship to do so without careful consideration. She was absolutely right. In response, we came up with a few rules, establishing when I should involve her and when she preferred not to be involved, what percentage of income I could operate in freely before needing to consult with her, and so on. I'm glad for these now—our guidelines honor her, keep me more mindful, and allow us both to operate as the Lord has called us to financially.

For many years, Doris and I didn't pray together—not when we were considering major purchases, and not when we were looking to make a donation. Now, to pray together over these things while mutually seeking God's will is one of our greatest joys. Once we've heard each other out, our prayers become even more meaningful, further connecting us on a more intimate level and drawing us closer to the Lord. This gives us a productive and emotionally safe way to move together through hard conversations and tough decisions.

Not all couples are comfortable praying together in moments of decision or disagreement. But it's invaluable for me to have a wife who will pray with me and seek God's desires for my life and for whom I can do the same. And when our prayers are about giving, we get to enjoy God's "gift of giving"—the excitement of being able to give together.

Sometimes the Lord multiplies what we give in unexpected ways. At a Young Life camp that we visited several years ago, they were going to offer Bibles to new believers—but charge four dollars. Because Doris and I did not want new believers to have to purchase access to God's Word, we said we would donate the funds to make the Bibles available for free. The camp director misunderstood and told the organization's leadership that we would do this for *all* their camps nationwide. Though we hadn't intended a ministry-wide funding, Doris and I decided that is what the Lord wanted, and so we donated Bibles for many years.

This is very much what I mean by "Watch for circumstances" (Step 3). Doris and I were carried along by circumstances in that situation, but it was great because we could see the Lord's hand in it. And wherever His hand is, we want our hearts (and hands) to follow.

Planned Giving

I think God asks this kind of openness of all His children. Yes, there will be times when He prompts us to give spontaneously or beyond what we expected—and maybe to a ministry that we've never even considered before. Regardless, if you bring your stewardship decisions to Him, God will reveal His plans.

Obviously, you can invest in ministry with your time as well. Volunteering, serving on a board, spreading the word about what an organization is doing—these are other ways to give sacrificially. For each area of ministry that I either serve in or donate to, I try to regularly assess my involvement and whether I should do more or do something different. I take the time for this inventory because our callings do sometimes change as we enter new seasons. This was true for the men and women of the Bible; therefore, we shouldn't be surprised that it happens to us.

For example, there have been a few times over the years when I've realized I've lost my passion for serving on a board, and I have resigned—but not before consulting with the Lord and my wife about whether I should step off. I also process through the four steps with any of my personal principles that aren't specified in Scripture. To predetermine too many things, even things that seem "Christian," can be stifling to my relationship with Jesus. The key is to hold all my plans loosely in case the Lord wants to alter them. After all, He may choose to work, or have me work, differently than in the past. This is why I often have to approach my plans for giving (or anything else) as if I'm a two-year-old who knows virtually nothing about what's best.

Our Principles Versus God's Commands

Oswald Chambers wrote that there's a vast difference between devotion to a person (Jesus) and devotion to principles or to a cause.[1] If we're not careful, our personal principles can take on a life of their own—to where we start to uphold them as if they're biblical commands.

Once the Lord opened my eyes to my true stewardship passion, which is liberating souls, I started directing more time and money toward ministries with this focus. But not so long ago, I took it a step further (without consulting the Lord first) and decided I would only donate to discipleship ministries. However, Doris and I could not get peace about *not* giving to a camp for disabled kids. Once I surrendered my resolve of giving only to discipleship, we felt great peace about donating to that camp. I have since consulted God regarding all my principles—even that of donating a consistent percentage of my income. I never know; He might want a different percentage from me this year than He did last year!

We should stay true to Jesus' commands, such as "Love your enemy" and "Give generously." However, He did not say, "Give generously only to discipleship ministries." So we also need to offer up our causes until we've gotten neutral. I used to wonder, for example, if donating to efforts that weren't overtly Christian (such as the work that hospitals and universities do) was un-Christian. But as I studied the life of Jesus and prayed for Him to show me His answer, I figured out that mindset was not of Him.

To lock in on a principle of our own making will cause us to have blind spots and miss what Jesus has in store. It's also easier to compulsively overtry rather than operating peacefully, joyfully, fruitfully, and freely, as we would if we kept our eyes on Jesus. Our direction has to come from Him and His Word, not from our legalism or good intentions.

Remember, God sees the future; He cares about where we donate our money and everyone who receives it more than we do; and He knows best. So let's keep bringing Him our principles and our plans for giving and asking: "Lord, what would You have me do? Where should this money go?" If the answer comes from having patiently sought His will, you can be confident that He has guided you to send it where He intends it.

EPILOGUE

....

THE BOTTOM LINE

F OR TWO ENTIRE YEARS awhile back, I wanted to quit
giving away half my income so I could, as I viewed it, have more
money. In my case, it was a control issue: I reasoned that if I kept those
funds in my pocket, Texon wouldn't need to borrow money on someone
else's terms. Plus, I would have more cash for any unforeseen problems.

Hearing this, you might expect that this struggle cropped up after
a major financial loss. No. It happened at a time of extreme success.

I had been giving away fifty percent of my income for better than
a decade when Texon finally sold a major division. I now had less
stress and more cash, but for the first time in all those years, I hesi-
tated to donate so much. A year later we sold an even larger division,
so I had even less stress and more money. In spite of that, the desire to
cut my giving only intensified.

Though in the end I didn't change my level of giving, you should
have heard all my excuses and rationalizations! What's amazing to
me in retrospect is that it took me so long to see what was happening.
I was still practicing my daily spiritual disciplines, I'd been slowing
down and waiting on God for more than twenty years, and the Lord
had brought me to a place of no personal or corporate asset debt—yet
I quit trusting Him. I wanted to keep more for myself. Rely on myself.

While it's not unusual for any of us to struggle in this way after

197

an asset sale or windfall (such as an inheritance or a job bonus), that's exactly the time to stick to your commitments. I feel blessed because the Holy Spirit peeled off my blinders before I did anything stupid. He showed me that I was failing to trust; He reminded me that only the Lord is in control, and we are actually in control of nothing. I confessed, moved through the four steps, and was finally able to hear the clear voice of God concerning my giving—and continue giving away the 50 percent joyfully. It was a classic example of, "Never assume you've mastered your past sins." It also perfectly illustrates how difficult it is not only to surrender to the Lord but to remain surrendered.

Small Deaths That Lead to Life

Throughout this book, I have referred to my process of finding the Lord's will about important decisions using phrases such as "slowing down to a sacred pace," "getting neutral," and "waiting on the Lord." In this quest to trust Him instead of myself, I am constantly seeking to surrender my will to His. In theological terms, it is called "dying to self"—and it is the real bottom line of this book.

Just as it sounds, dying to oneself is very hard. No one understands just how hard it is until they have actually succeeded by fully offering up a deep desire (or perhaps someone they really love) to God. We must die to any idol or any influence that wants to push Jesus out of the driver's seat. This includes the influence of others and even our concern about what will happen to somebody else if we heed God's answer. (It helps in these instances to remind yourself that the Lord knows what's best for your loved ones too, and He cares for them in ways that you can't.)

Archbishop Fenelon said it well:

Whatever spiritual knowledge or feelings we may have, they are all a delusion if they do not lead us to the real and constant practice of dying to self. And it is true that we do not die without suffering. Nor is it possible to be considered truly dead while there is any part of us which is yet alive. This spiritual death (which is really a blessing in disguise) is undeniably painful. It cuts swift and deep into our innermost thoughts and desires with all their parts, exposing us for what we really are. The Great Physician who sees in us what we cannot see, knows exactly where to place the knife. He cuts away that which we are most reluctant to give up. And how it hurts! But we must remember that pain is only felt where there is life, and where there is life is just the place where death is needed. . . . Do not misunderstand me; [our Father] wants you to live abundantly, but this can only be accomplished by allowing Him to cut into that fleshly part of you which is still stubbornly clinging to life.[1]

Happily, our story with Jesus never ends in death. These "small deaths" open up into life overflowing with God's wisdom and grace. While the process may not be painless, we can expect God to be good—and to be greater than our suffering. And the process is effective: you *will* learn God's will if you'll slow down and surrender your earthly desires.

Dying to self is a blessed bottom line that yields huge returns of joy and peace and intimacy with Jesus. It also breaks us open to receive what we want most: God's best for us.

But you can't do it without faith in Someone greater; otherwise, there's no one to die to. Here's the upside, though: in an interesting twist that has become even clearer to me in the writing of this book, when you die to self is exactly when the Lord reveals Himself. And suddenly you don't just see the desires of your heart, you *receive* them!

Oswald Chambers described our dilemma well: "We want the witness [God's revelation] before we have done what God tells us to do. 'Why does God not reveal Himself to me?'" Chambers replies: "He cannot, because you are in the way as long as you won't abandon absolutely to Him." But as soon as you give up yourself, God makes Himself known in you through the power of the Holy Spirit.[2] His will and your delight become apparent.

It is hard to explain this exchange, and it is hard to believe until you've experienced it, but once you have died to your fleshly desires, God is faithful to fulfill the longings of your heart—and the answers to your biggest decisions.

A Divine Dividend

Dying to self doesn't mean you have no preference about the answer you receive; it does mean you get to where, *in spite of your preference*, your strongest desire is to discover and do God's will. That is when God has you where He wants you. That is the point at which you will receive His answer and the peace that accompanies it.

This aspect of dying to self always reminds me of Jesus in the Garden of Gethsemane before His crucifixion. Matthew 26:39 records His prayer: "My Father, if it is possible, may this cup be taken from me. Yet not as I will, but as you will." God's own Son—His own Son!—clearly had a preference, but He was willing to give up His wishes for God's greater purpose. Jesus not only died to self, but He gave His life in pursuit of His Father's will!

What was the divine dividend? Hebrews 12:2 indicates that Jesus received the desires of His heart: "For the joy set before him he endured the cross . . . and sat down at the right hand of the throne of God."

Who's Driving?

Here's a true story to bring us to our destination for this book. One of my closest friends has a friend, Curtis, who once picked up a hitch-hiker out in California.

"Hop in the back," Curtis told him.

"I'd like to come up front," the hitchhiker said. Curtis wasn't sensing any danger, so he invited the guy to join him. Before long, though, the guy admitted, "I'd really like to drive."

It's hard for us to fathom someone being so brazen, and yet, that's often how we are with the Lord. We either want Him in the backseat or navigating, but not driving. According to Curtis, when it comes to our lives, "We really have to be honest about who's driving." Like Curtis's hitchhiker, it also wouldn't hurt to be honest about our desire to drive.

Who's driving your life and decisions? Just as importantly: Who's the best one to do the driving? And what speed does the Expert recommend for the road you're on?

I like the way John Piper sums up the risks and rewards of the Christian life: "Disobedience is always a greater risk than obedience." I could add to that, "Demanding our way is always a greater risk than letting God have His way." Romans 4:20–21 tells us Abraham "grew strong in his faith as he gave glory to God, fully convinced that God was able to do what he had promised" (ESV).

I hope that as several of us have shared our experiences of getting neutral, you've become convinced in your soul that the rewards of consulting God for your important decisions far exceed the risks. I also hope you now know in your heart that God can be trusted and that He is good. If you have these assurances in you, you're positioned to experience His best in your business, your household, your relationships, and your life, for in Him "are hidden all the treasures of wisdom and knowledge" (Col. 2:3, ESV).

Get ready! Because when you look to the Lord and trust His timing, you receive not just His decisions and His desires, but *your* heart's desires. Most of all, you get more of Him—and He never, ever disappoints.

NOTES

Chapter 2: The Crash

1. John Piper, *Future Grace: The Purifying Power of the Promises of God*, rev. ed. (Colorado Springs, CO: Multnomah, 2012), 313.

Chapter 3: A Way to His Will

1. *Why Go to Work?* Ministry in the Marketplace Series (Colorado Springs, CO: Ministry in the Marketplace, 1987; reprint, 2010).
2. *Why Go to Work?*, 8.

Chapter 4: My First Test Run

1. George Müller, quoted in Michael F. Bird, *Romans, The Story of God Bible Commentary*; gen eds. Tremper Longman III and Scot McKnight (Grand Rapids, MI: Zondervan, 2016), cxxxii, emphasis mine.

Chapter 5: In Step with God

1. Description of the Garmin Approach S6 Golf Watch in "The Holiday Help List," *Sports Illustrated*, December 1, 2014, https://www.si.com/vault/2014/12/01/106676816/the-holiday-help-list.
2. Tim Keller, personal correspondence with the author, October 18, 2017. Used by permission.

3. Chris Tiegreen, "Rock of Wisdom," *The One Year Walk with God Devotional: Wisdom from the Bible to Renew Your Mind* (Carol Stream, IL: Tyndale, 2004), October 15 reading.

4. Tiegreen, *One Year Walk with God Devotional*, October 15 reading.

5. Sharon Salzberg, "The Power of Patience," *Awakin.org*, February 10, 2014, http://www.awakin.org/read/view.php?tid=977.

6. John Owen, *The Works of John Owen*, ed. Thomas Russell (London: Richard Baynes, 1826), 3:187.

Chapter 6: Trust and Believe

1. Bill Blocker, personal correspondence with the author, October 11, 2017. Used by permission.

2. Chris Tiegreen, "Rock of Wisdom," *The One Year Walk with God Devotional: Wisdom from the Bible to Renew Your Mind* (Carol Stream, IL: Tyndale, 2004), October 15 reading.

3. John Patchell, interview with the author, July 14, 2015. Used by permission.

4. Jon Bloom, "The Insanity of Leaning on Our Own Understanding," Desiring God, March 7, 2014, http://www.desiringgod.org/articles/the-insanity-of-leaning-on-our-own-understanding.

5. Tiegreen, "The Escape from Self," *One Year Walk with God Devotional*, March 15 reading.

6. Tiegreen, "Praying God's Mind," *One Year Walk with God Devotional*, October 22 reading.

7. John Ortberg, *All the Places to Go . . . How Will You Know?* (Carol Stream, IL: Tyndale House, 2015), 121.

8. Thanks to Pastor Jon Sterns, Vineyard Church of Franklin, TN, for this definition of *faith*.

Chapter 7: Step 1: Consult Your Friend Jesus

1. Charles Stanley, *The Power of God's Love: A 31-Day Devotional to Encounter the Father's Greatest Gift* (Nashville: Thomas Nelson, 2008), 101.

2. Stanley, *The Power of God's Love*, 101.

3. Annie F. Downs, Instagram post, May 31, 2018, https://www
.instagram.com/p/BjcdR1wA9G4/?taken-by=anniefdowns.

4. John Piper, *Desiring God: Meditations of a Christian Hedonist*
(Colorado Springs, CO: Multnomah, 2011), 162.

5. Oswald Chambers, "Friendship with God," *My Utmost for His Highest*
(Grand Rapids, MI: Discovery House, 1963), March 20 reading.

6. Norman Vincent Peale, *The Power of Positive Thinking* (New York:
Fireside, 1980), 6.

7. Pierre Teilhard de Chardin, quoted in Charles R. Swindoll, *The Tale
of the Tardy Oxcart: And 1,501 Other Stories* (Nashville, TN: Word,
1998), 322.

Chapter 8: Step 2: Gather the Facts

1. Howard Thurman, quoted by John Eldredge in "What Makes You
Come Alive?" FaithGateway blog, October 12, 2016, http://www.
faithgateway.com/makes-come-alive-2/#.WV47r__yufR.

2. Chris Tiegreen, "The Escape from Self," *The One Year Walk with God
Devotional: Wisdom from the Bible to Renew Your Mind* (Carol Stream,
IL: Tyndale, 2004), March 15 reading.

Chapter 9: Step 3: Watch for Circumstances

1. George Müller, quoted in *Living with Power*, Operation Timothy
Classic, vol. 3 (Chattanooga, TN: CBMC, 1995), 36.

Chapter 10: Step 4: Get Neutral

1. Oswald Chambers, "Something More about His Ways," *My Utmost
for His Highest* (Grand Rapids, MI: Discovery House, 1963), August 1
reading.

2. Chambers, "Dependent on God's Presence," *My Utmost*, July 20
reading, emphasis mine.

3. Crawford Loritts, quoted in *GriefShare: Your Journey from Mourning
to Joy*, 3rd ed. (Wake Forest, NC: Church Initiative, 2016), 129.

4. Chambers, "The Overshadowing Personal Deliverance," *My Utmost*,
June 27 reading.

5. Quoted in Chris Tiegreen, "God's Good Favor," *The One Year Walk with God Devotional* (Carol Stream, IL: Tyndale, 2004), June 6 reading.

6. George Müller, quoted in *Living with Power*, Operation Timothy Classic, vol. 3 (Chattanooga, TN: CBMC, 1995), 36.

7. George Whitefield, "On the Method of Grace," in *The World's Famous Orations* (Great Britain: 1906), 1:710–1777, https://www.bartleby.com/268/3/20.html.

8. Francois Fenelon in Gene Edwards, "Let Go of Anxiety," *100 Days in the Secret Place: Classic Writings from Madame Guyon, Francois Fenelon, and Michael Molinos on the Deeper Christian Life* (Shippensburg, PA: Destiny Image, 2015), 87.

9. Francois Fenelon, *The Seeking Heart*, Library of Spiritual Classics, vol. 4 (Sargent, GA: SeedSowers, 1992), 81.

10. Henry Blackaby, *Experiencing God* (Nashville: B&H, 2008), 32.

11. Fenelon, *The Seeking Heart*, 63.

12. Müller, *Living with Power*, 36.

Chapter 11: Is It the Holy Spirit or Intuition?

1. Oswald Chambers, "Faith," *My Utmost for His Highest* (Uhrichsville, OH: Barbour, 2000), October 30 reading.

2. Quoted in Charles Stanley, "An Absolute Essential," *Pathways to His Presence: A Daily Devotional* (Nashville: Thomas Nelson, 2006), November 9 reading.

3. Personal correspondence with the author, February 2016. Used by permission.

4. Tim Keller, personal correspondence with author, October 18, 2017. Used by permission.

5. Francois Fenelon, *Let Go* (New Kensington, PA: Whitaker House, 1973), 9.

Chapter 13: How Can I Help Myself Stop the Hurrying?

1. Francois Fenelon, *The Seeking Heart*, Library of Spiritual Classics, vol. 4 (Sargent, GA: SeedSowers, 1992), 84.

2. Matthew Henry, *Matthew Henry's Concise Commentary*, Bible Hub, accessed February 18, 2017, http://biblehub.com/commentaries/mhc/romans/12.htm.

Chapter 14: Pain Is Not the Enemy

1. Francois Fenelon, *The Seeking Heart*, Library of Spiritual Classics vol. 4 (Sargent, GA: SeedSowers, 1992), 52.
2. Francois Fenelon in Gene Edwards, "The Hidden Cross," *100 Days in the Secret Place: Classic Writings from Madame Guyon, Francois Fenelon, and Michael Molinos on the Deeper Christian Life* (Shippensburg, PA: Destiny Image, 2015), 33.
3. Fenelon, "The Value of the Cross," *100 Days*, 34.

Chapter 15: Are They God's Desires or Mine?

1. Matthew Henry, *Matthew Henry's Concise Commentary*, Bible Hub, accessed February 18, 2017, http://biblehub.com/commentaries/mhc/romans/12.htm
2. John Ortberg, *Soul Keeping* (Grand Rapids, MI: Zondervan, 2014).
3. John Patchell, interview with the author, July 14, 2015. Used by permission.

Chapter 16: With Your Spouse

1. Boyd Bailey, "Praying Husband," WisdomHunters.com, accessed February 25, 2018, https://www.wisdomhunters.com/praying-husband-3/.

Chapter 18: While at Work

1. Brian Solomon, "Meet David Green: Hobby Lobby's Biblical Billionaire," *Forbes*, September 18, 2012; http://www.forbes.com/sites/briansolomon/2012/09/18/david-green-the-biblical-billionaire-backing-the-evangelical-movement.
2. Laurie Beth Jones has a great book, *The Path: Creating Your Mission Statement for Work and for Life* (New York: Hachette, 1996), to help anyone develop a personal mission statement.

Notes

Chapter 20: In Ministry and Giving

1. Oswald Chambers, "The Conditions of Discipleship," *My Utmost for His Highest* (Uhrichsville, OH: Barbour, 2000), July 2 reading.

Epilogue

1. Francois Fenelon, *Let Go: To Get Peace and Real Joy,* "Letter 4: The Death of Self" (New Kensington, PA: Whitaker House, 1973), 6–7.
2. Oswald Chambers, "The Witness of the Spirit," *My Utmost for His Highest* (Uhrichsville, OH: Barbour, 2000), October 22 reading.

ACKNOWLEDGMENTS

T O SEALY YATES, MY faithful and spiritual book agent. He gave me the clarity and conviction for the theme of the book and was relentless in pursuing a great publisher.

To Kris Bearss, my tireless collaborative writer. She was a great partner and strategic thinker who provided amazing organization of the chapters and subject matter. I am indebted to Kris as she also drew clarity of key points from my soul.

To the team at W Publishing and HarperCollins Christian Publishing, who made major contributions to the content and the final product.

To my family, friends, employees, and the ministry leaders who invested their time, thoughts, and prayers in helping make *Sacred Pace* the book it is.

And lastly but most importantly, to my wife, Doris, who was so faithful to read and invest in all the many manuscripts and drafts. I am grateful for her encouragement, patience, and honesty, helping me see the truth time and time again.

ABOUT THE AUTHOR

TERRY LOOPER is married to Doris, his wife of fifty years, and has two married daughters and five grandchildren. The founder of Texon LP—one of Houston's top privately owned revenue producers and an industry leader in customer retention—he has served as the company's president and chief executive officer for thirty years and has previously been named an Ernst & Young Regional Entrepreneur of the Year. In his mission to see souls liberated for God's kingdom, Terry sits on multiple nonprofit boards and is deeply committed to mentoring and discipleship.

A seminary-trained, award-winning writer and editor, **KRIS BEARSS** is a former Christian publishing executive who now freelances full-time. During her thirty years in the industry, she has been involved in several significant Bible projects, including the *ESV Study Bible* and the *Jeremiah Study Bible,* and has worked collaboratively or editorially with dozens of bestselling authors such as David Jeremiah, Andy Stanley, Sarah Young, Beth Moore, Max Lucado, and Stephen Arterburn. She is also a Bible teacher and speaker with a lifelong passion for helping to raise up next-generation leaders in the church and culture.